How You Can Be In The Perfect Will Of God

by

Dag Heward-Mills

A part of the "Work of Ministry" series

HOW YOU CAN BE IN THE PERFECT WILL OF GOD

Copyright © 2013 by Dag Heward-Mills

The right of Dag Heward-Mills to be identified as the author of this work has been asserted in accordance with the Copyright, Designs and Patents Act 1988.

All Rights reserved under international copyright law. No part of this publication may be reproduced, stored in a retrieval system, or transmitted, in any form or by any means without the prior written consent of the publisher and copyright owner, nor be otherwise circulated in any form of binding or cover other than that in which it is published and without a similar condition being imposed on the subsequent purchaser. Written permission must be secured from the publisher to use or reproduce any part of this book, except for brief quotations in critical reviews or articles.

Unless otherwise stated, all Scripture quotations are taken from the King James Version of the Bible.

ISBN # 978-1-909278-78-3

First published in Great Britain in 2013 by ChristLight Books
www.christlightbooks.com
(Sunpenny Publishing Group)

evangelist@daghewardmills.org
www.daghewardmills.org

Write to:
P.O. Box 114, Korle-Bu, Accra, Ghana

BOOKS IN THE "WORK OF MINISTRY" SERIES:

Losing, Suffering, Sacrificing, Dying
Many Are Called
Proton
Rules Of Church Work
Rules Of Full-Time Ministry

Contents

1. The Perfect Will and the Imperfect Will of God 1
2. Understanding How People Enter the Imperfect Will of God 15
3. Why There Are So Many People in the Imperfect Will of God 21
4. The Mysterious Will of God 27
5. Be Filled with the Knowledge of His Will 35
6. Twenty Reasons Why You Must Be Led by the Spirit of God 51
7. Twelve Different Kinds of Voices 79
8. The Voice of the Bible 93
9. Five Keys to Victory over the Voice of Your Flesh .. 101
10. Three Things You Should Know about the Voice of the Holy Spirit 107
11. Seven Characteristics of the Inner Witness 113
12. How to Use "Peace the Umpire" for Daily Guidance 117

13. How to Tell the Difference When the Spirit Speaks in Different Ways 121
14. Four Reasons for Spectacular Guidance 127
15. How to Identify a Door 133
16. What Every Christian Should Know about Dreams.. 141
17. How to Interpret Different Kinds of Dreams 147
18. How to Relate to a Prophet 153
19. The Secret of Directed Paths 163
20. How to Deal with the Voice of the People 167
21. How Not to Be Led by Circumstances 173
22. How to Unmask the Devil 177
23. Three Checks to Avoiding Mistakes When Being Led by the Spirit 181
24. Why You Must Listen to Your Conscience 189
25. Twelve Levels of Obedience to the Lord 193
26. Common Alternatives to Obedience 205
27. The Promises and Blessings for Obedience 217

How You Can Be In The Perfect Will Of God

Chapter 1

The Perfect Will and the Imperfect Will of God

> ... that ye may prove what is that good, and acceptable, and PERFECT, WILL OF GOD.
>
> **Romans 12:2**

The will of God can be described as being perfect or imperfect. The imperfect will of God is called imperfect because it has the semblance of the true will of God but is not really what God wants.

The perfect will of God is the complete, mature and full will of God. The imperfect will of God is what God allows men to do even though it is not His first choice for them.

The Perfect Will of God

1. The perfect will of God is the place where God really wants you to be. God is pleased with you when you are in His perfect will and He is excited when your name is mentioned.

2. In the perfect will of God you are excellently positioned, fitting exactly into the original plan of God.

3. In the perfect will of God, you perfectly meet the needs for which God designed you.

The Imperfect Will of God

1. God allows His children into the imperfect will as a result of their rebelliousness and rejection of His original and perfect plan for them.

2. When you are in the imperfect will of God, God is not really pleased with you. He is just accommodating you, being patient with you and giving you time to repent.

3. In the imperfect will of God you may seem to have God's favour but you are incomplete in your service to the Lord and not fulfilling God's original purpose for your life.

4. The imperfect will of God is the place where you are inappropriately positioned and also un-qualified for your job.

Moving from the Perfect to the Imperfect Will of God

All through the Bible, you will find examples of God allowing men to do what they wanted to do even though it was not His perfect will for them. Most of the time, God's people were full of rebellion and hatred for the perfect will of God. Instead of passing an immediate judgment, God would allow His people to stray into His imperfect (inappropriate, improper, unacceptable, non-ideal) will and then receive a sound and fitting thrashing for their rebelliousness!

In this book, you will discover how God allows people to have a king but uses kings to punish them. He allows people to have prosperity but then sends delusions and leanness into their souls. He allows people to build idols and then destroys them.

He allows a prophet to go on a mission, but then sends a donkey to rebuke him.

God does not contradict Himself by allowing people to stray into His imperfect will. It is His response to the rebellion, stubbornness and rejection of His perfect will. In the end, all men receive the appropriate, well-tailored and innovative judgments of God!

Some people call this imperfect will the permissive will of God. This imperfect will of God is the place where many ministers of the gospel function. Some people live their whole lives in this imperfect will of God.

Everything seems to be alright with people in the imperfect will of God. Their ministries flourish and the favour of God seems to be upon everything they do. But abundance and apparent success does not mean that God is pleased with you.

Most of us are deceived by apparent favour and what people call "blessings".

Money and abundance has never been a sign that God is pleased with you. The devil also gives money to those who serve him. Satan told Jesus to bow down and he would give Him the whole world.

God's presence and the voice of the Holy Spirit are what you must look for and not the presence of money or anything physical.

When you come into contact with a minister you must look to see if the presence of God is with him. You must watch to see if the voice of God and the Word of the Lord are present.

The Bible is littered with examples of God's people moving away from the perfect will of God and into the imperfect will of God. God seems to be blessing people who are in the imperfect will of God but He is not really pleased with them.

Let us look at some of the examples of people moving into the imperfect will of God.

1. Israel entered the imperfect will of God by insisting on having a king.

Having a king was not the perfect, mature wish of God for Israel. But God granted it to them and told Samuel privately that the people had rejected Him.

Having a king was not the perfect will of God and yet God allowed it. As you will discover, this arrangement did not turn out well and the children of Israel suffered greatly under their kings.

It is important not to be deceived when God apparently allows certain things. The true heart of God is revealed to people who are genuinely close to Him.

We do that all the time, saying what is politically right when we are in public but revealing our true hearts elsewhere. You must learn to seek God's real mind and heart on a matter.

The Lord was grieved when He allowed Samuel to appoint a king. He knew He had been rejected by the people. He knew the people were just using Samuel's sons as an excuse for rejecting Him. God consented to their request but all would not be well with Israel. Watch out for when God seems to allow things in your life that He really does not want.

> *Then all the elders of Israel gathered themselves together, and came to Samuel unto Ramah,*
>
> *And said unto him, Behold, thou art old, and thy sons walk not in thy ways: now make us a king to judge us like all the nations.*

> *But the thing displeased Samuel, when they said, Give us a king to judge us. And Samuel prayed unto the Lord.*
>
> *And the Lord said unto Samuel, Hearken unto the voice of the people in all that they say unto thee: for they have not rejected thee, but they have rejected me, that I should not reign over them.*
>
> **1 Samuel 8:4-7**

2. Balaam moved out of the perfect will of God when he continued to request for a chance to prophesy to the king of Moab.

The Lord had made it clear to Balaam that He did not want him to have anything to do with Balak the king of Moab. However, Balaam really wanted to have some of the money that Balak had offered. He pressed the Lord into allowing him to speak to the king. In the end, the Lord said he should go. The Lord even gave him advice on how to speak to them. Modern Christians would have taken this to mean it was the will of God. This passage is there to warn us that God will seem to allow us to do our own thing when He knows that we are filled with rebellion.

> *Then God came to Balaam and said, "Who are these men with you?"*
>
> *And Balaam said to God, "Balak the son of Zippor, king of Moab, has sent word to me,*
>
> *'Behold, there is a people who came out of Egypt and they cover the surface of the land; now come, curse*

them for me; perhaps I may be able to fight against them, and drive them out.'

AND GOD SAID TO BALAAM, "DO NOT GO WITH THEM; YOU SHALL NOT CURSE THE PEOPLE; FOR THEY ARE BLESSED."

So Balaam arose in the morning and said to Balak's leaders, "Go back to your land, for the Lord has refused to let me go with you."

And the leaders of Moab arose and went to Balak, and said, "Balaam refused to come with us."

Then Balak again sent leaders, more numerous and more distinguished than the former.

And they came to Balaam and said to him, "Thus says Balak the son of Zippor, 'Let nothing, I beg you, hinder you from coming to me; for I will indeed honor you richly, and I will do whatever you say to me. Please come then, curse this people for me.'"

And Balaam answered and said to the servants of Balak, "Though Balak were to give me his house full of silver and gold, I could not do anything, either small or great, contrary to the command of the Lord my God."

"And now please, you also stay here tonight, and I will find out what else the Lord will speak to me."

AND GOD CAME TO BALAAM AT NIGHT AND SAID TO HIM, "IF THE MEN HAVE COME TO CALL YOU, RISE UP AND GO WITH THEM; BUT ONLY THE WORD WHICH I SPEAK TO YOU SHALL YOU DO."

So Balaam arose in the morning, and saddled his donkey, and went with the leaders of Moab.

BUT GOD WAS ANGRY BECAUSE HE WAS GOING, and the angel of the lord took his stand in the way as an adversary against him. Now he was riding on his donkey and his two servants were with him.

Numbers 22:9-22 (NASB)

3. The children of Israel moved out of the perfect will of God when they lusted after prosperity.

They soon forgat his works; they waited not for his counsel: But lusted exceedingly in the wilderness, and tempted God in the desert.

And he gave them their request; but sent leanness into their soul.

Psalms 106:13-15

The children of Israel, just like the modern church, lusted after money. Just as it happened in those days, the Lord gave them prosperity preachers who used the Word to legitimize their craving for earthly things.

The continuous over-emphasis on the preaching of prosperity with its attendant glamour seems to be the will of God. The presence of large crowds and the apparent success of many ministries give the impression that God is happy with everything.

It seemed that God had answered the Israelites' desire for prosperity but they were in the imperfect will of God because God punished them for lusting after prosperity. And the punishment was a *leanness of their soul.*

God would not have punished them if they were doing the right thing.

God wants His children to prosper but not in the wrong way and for the wrong reasons. He granted them prosperity because He is not against prosperity. Today, God is granting prosperity to His church but it seems it is accompanied by a leanness of soul, spiritual shallowness, disease, divorce, immorality and homosexuality. Let us be careful of what we force God to give us because we may not be happy with the attendant punishments that go with insisting on our own way.

4. The children of Israel entered the imperfect will of God when they forced Aaron to make a calf.

The children of Israel seemed to have their own way as they demanded that Aaron make gods to lead them.

As Aaron made the calf for them, they must have thought that God had started a new religion that involved idol worship.

The Israelites revelled in their new religion assuming that God had approved of them because of Aaron's involvement.

But they were not in the will of God even though God's man seemed to have led them. It was not long before they reaped the punishment of being in the imperfect will of God.

And when the people saw that Moses delayed to come down out of the mount, the people gathered themselves together unto Aaron, and said unto him, Up, make us gods, which shall go before us; for as for this Moses, the man that brought us up out of the land of Egypt, we wot not what is become of him.

And Aaron said unto them, Break off the golden earrings, which are in the ears of your wives, of your sons, and of your daughters, and bring them unto me.

And all the people brake off the golden earrings which were in their ears, and brought them unto Aaron.

And he received them at their hand, and fashioned it with a graving tool, after he had made it a molten calf: and they said, These be thy gods, O Israel, which brought thee up out of the land of Egypt.

Exodus 32:1-4

They made a calf in Horeb, and worshipped the molten image.

Thus they changed their glory into the similitude of an ox that eateth grass.

They forgat God their saviour, which had done great things in Egypt;

Wondrous works in the land of Ham, and terrible things by the Red sea.

Therefore he said that he would destroy them, had not Moses his chosen stood before him in the breach, to turn away his wrath, lest he should destroy them.

Psalms 106:19-23

5. Nadab and Abihu were in the imperfect will of God when they offered a sacrifice that God had not asked for.

Offering sacrifices to the Lord is a good thing to do. And that is exactly what Nadab and Abihu did. They offered sacrifices to the Lord but God was not pleased with them. They actually died because of this. Once again, we see people doing good things but receiving punishment for it because it was not the perfect will of God.

> *And Nadab and Abihu, the sons of Aaron, took either of them his censer, and put fire therein, and put incense thereon, and offered strange fire before the Lord, which he commanded them not.*
>
> *And there went out fire from the Lord, and devoured them, and they died before the Lord.*
>
> **Leviticus 10:1-2**

6. Abraham entered the imperfect will of God when he produced an heir through Hagar.

Abraham introduced all kinds of problems into his life by having a child with Hagar. God did not tell him to have a child with Hagar but he wanted to please his wife.

God allowed him to marry Hagar and even blessed Hagar's child. But that was not the perfect will of God. God had told him that He was going to make him the father of many nations through Sarai.

Now Sarai Abram's wife bare him no children: and she had an handmaid, an Egyptian, whose name was Hagar.

And Sarai said unto Abram, Behold now, the LORD hath restrained me from bearing: I pray thee, go in unto my maid; it may be that I may obtain children by her. And Abram hearkened to the voice of Sarai.

Genesis 16:1-2

7. The children of Israel moved out of the perfect will of God when He allowed them to divorce.

God never intended for us to divorce. But He seemed to allow and even bless polygamous marriages in the Old Testament.

There are many people who believe that polygamous marriages are biblical because all the patriarchs had polygamous marriages. So why did God seem to have an ambivalent attitude towards divorce and remarriage in the Old Testament?

When the question of divorce came up, Jesus settled the matter once and for all. He revealed the perfect will of God. He showed us that God did not really approve of divorce and remarriage.

In the Old Testament, God seemed to have approved of divorce but it was simply His response to the hardness of the hearts of the people.

Remember that in the perfect will of God, you fit into His original plan for you. His original plan was not divorce. God allowed it because He recognized that the people's hearts were hardened. God may seem to be allowing certain things in your life and ministry. Perhaps it is because your heart is hardened.

> *And some Pharisees came up to Him, testing Him, and began to question Him whether it was lawful for a man to divorce a wife.*
>
> *And He answered and said to them, "What did Moses command you?"*
>
> *And they said, "Moses permitted a man to write a certificate of divorce and send her away."*
>
> *But Jesus said to them, "Because of your hardness of heart he wrote you this commandment.*
>
> *But from the beginning of creation, God made them male and female.*
>
> *For this cause a man shall leave his father and mother, and the two shall become one flesh; consequently they are no longer two, but one flesh.*
>
> *What therefore God has joined together, let no man separate."*
>
> **Mark 10:2-9 (NASB)**

Chapter 2

Understanding How People Enter the Imperfect Will of God

So then do not be foolish, but UNDERSTAND what the will of the Lord is.

Ephesians 5:17 (NASB)

1. **People enter the imperfect will of God by not accurately hearing the voice of God.**

   Now SAMUEL DID NOT YET KNOW THE LORD, NEITHER WAS THE WORD OF THE LORD YET REVEALED UNTO HIM.

   1 Samuel 3:7

It is important to be able to hear when God speaks. If you cannot tell when God has spoken then you are going to be in serious trouble. That is why the art of hearing

God's voice is crucial to your survival. It is only when you have developed the art of hearing that you can be in the perfect will of God. Many people are in the imperfect will of God because they *do not* and *cannot* hear when God speaks.

2. People enter the imperfect will of God because God allows men to have a free will.

> *But as many as received him, to them gave he power to become the sons of God, even to them that believe on his name:*
>
> **John 1:12**

Amazingly, God does not force anyone to love Him or serve Him. God respects your will or decision to go to Heaven or to Hell. If you decide to do something against His will He will respect your decision and allow you to destroy yourself.

The prodigal son was allowed to leave home because the father knew better than to keep an unwilling and rebellious son at home. Jesus came to this world to save us all. But He respects the will of the people to accept His salvation or to reject Him. "And this is the condemnation, that light is come into the world, and men loved darkness rather than light, because their deeds were evil" (John 3:19).

People will be condemned because light came to the world but they freely chose the darkness.

3. People enter the imperfect will of God because they want to be like others.

Wanting to be like others is the most dangerous desire a man of God can have. Wanting to be like others will lead you to reject God and His will. Jesus said, "I receive not honour from men" (John 5:41).

> *Then all the elders of Israel gathered themselves together, and came to Samuel unto Ramah, And said unto him, Behold, thou art old, and thy sons walk not in thy ways: now make us a king to judge us LIKE ALL THE NATIONS*
>
> **1 Samuel 8:4-5**

4. People enter the imperfect will of God because they are presumptuous.

To be presumptuous is to arrogantly assume that privileges must be given to you. Uzziah wrongly assumed that because he was the king he had the right to do the work of priests. We often assume that we know the will of God because He has used us in the past. When we become presumptuous, we assume that our ideas are God's ideas and our will is God's will. Arrogance and pride lead us into error and into the imperfect will of God. No matter who you are you are still a man and your will is not necessarily God's will. You must seek the will of God.

> *But when he was strong, his heart was lifted up to his destruction: for he transgressed against the LORD his God, and went into the temple of the LORD to burn incense upon the altar of incense.*
>
> *And Azariah the priest went in after him, and with him fourscore priests of the LORD, that were valiant men:*
>
> *And they withstood Uzziah the king, and said unto him, It appertaineth not unto thee, Uzziah, to burn incense unto the LORD, but to the priests the sons of Aaron, that are consecrated to burn incense: go out of the sanctuary; for thou hast trespassed; neither shall it be for thine honour from the LORD God.*
>
> *Then Uzziah was wroth, and had a censer in his hand to burn incense: and while he was wroth with the priests, the leprosy even rose up in his forehead before the priests in the house of the LORD, from beside the incense altar.*
>
> *And Azariah the chief priest, and all the priests, looked upon him, and, behold, he was leprous in his forehead, and they thrust him out from thence; yea, himself hasted also to go out, because the LORD had smitten him.*
>
> **2 Chronicles 26:16-20**

5. People enter the imperfect will of God by resting too quickly.

Do not rejoice too quickly or assume the airs of a champion. This is the sure sign that you will be destroyed soon. David rested, and did not go out to war, even though it was a time for war. This single moment of relaxation caused him to enter into the imperfect will of God. The imperfect will of God became one of the darkest phases of his life and ministry.

> *And it came to pass, after the year was expired, at the time when kings go forth to battle, that David sent Joab, and his servants with him, and all Israel; and they destroyed the children of Ammon, and besieged Rabbah. But DAVID TARRIED STILL AT JERUSALEM.*
>
> **2 Samuel 11:1**

6. People enter the imperfect will of God because of their impatience.

Patiently waiting for the will of God will make you bear much fruit for the Lord.

If the people had patiently waited for Moses to come down from the mountain they would never have entered the forty-year wilderness phase of their lives.

Being in the wilderness for forty years was not the perfect will of God. Forty years in the wilderness was the imperfect will of God that was imposed on the children of Israel because of their impatience. May you be delivered from having a wilderness season thrust upon you because of impatience!

> WHEN THE PEOPLE SAW HOW LONG IT WAS TAKING Moses to come back down the mountain, they gathered around Aaron. "Come on," they said, "make us some gods who can lead us. We don't know what happened to this fellow Moses, who brought us here from the land of Egypt."
>
> **Exodus 32:1 (NLT)**

7. People enter the imperfect will of God because of human manipulation.

Trusting in God is not easy. We are often tempted to do something to change things. God knows best. You must trust Him and believe that all things work together for good.

> And Sarai said unto Abram, Behold now, the Lord hath restrained me from bearing: I pray thee, GO IN UNTO MY MAID; It may be that I may obtain children by her. And Abram hearkened to the voice of Sarai.
>
> **Genesis 16:2**

Chapter 3

Why There Are So Many People in the Imperfect Will of God

Many people find themselves in the imperfect will of God. This is because the perfect will of God is mysteriously close and parallel to the imperfect will of God. This means that the will of God and the imperfect will of God have such similarities that you would think they are one and the same thing. You will notice that the perfect will of God is almost identical to the imperfect will of God.

Mysteriously, they are not the same thing. In fact, they are very different. Although the imperfect will of God is close and parallel to the perfect will of God, the outcomes are very different. Notice these examples:

1. Mary and Martha:

Mary chose the perfect will of God but Martha chose the imperfect will of God. Mary chose the one thing that was needful but Martha chose to be a chef. Both Mary and

Martha were close to Jesus but Mary chose to listen to the Word. Both of them loved Jesus and had Him in their home. But Mary was different because she chose the Word and Martha chose the food. Mary chose the good part and Martha chose the okay part.

> *And she had a sister called MARY, which also SAT AT JESUS' FEET, AND HEARD HIS WORD.*
>
> *But MARTHA WAS CUMBERED ABOUT MUCH SERVING, and came to him, and said, Lord, dost thou not care that my sister hath left me to serve alone? Bid her therefore that she help me.*
>
> *And Jesus answered and said unto her, Martha, Martha, thou art careful and troubled about many things:*
>
> *But ONE THING IS NEEDFUL: AND MARY HATH CHOSEN THAT GOOD PART, which shall not be taken away from her.*
>
> **Luke 10:39-42**

2. The five wise virgins and the five foolish virgins:

On the outside the five foolish virgins looked exactly the same as the five wise virgins but they were very different people.

The five wise virgins were in the perfect will of God but the five foolish virgins were not in the perfect will of God. At the end of this parable we see the two groups of virgins going in different directions. The perfect will of God and the imperfect will of God may be close and parallel but they are very different. When you are in the imperfect will of God you will end up in a different place from those who are in the perfect will of God.

> *Then shall the kingdom of heaven be likened unto ten virgins, which took their lamps, and went forth to meet the bridegroom.*
>
> *And five of them were wise, and five were foolish.*
>
> *They that were foolish took their lamps, and took no oil with them:*
>
> *But the wise took oil in their vessels with their lamps.*
>
> **Matthew 25:1-4**

3. The two women at the mill:

The two women at the mill looked like they were both in the perfect will of God. In the end, one of them was left behind and the other was taken to Heaven. How could that be? Although they looked the same, they were actually very different. Such is the mysterious will of God. It looks similar to the imperfect will of God but is indeed very different.

> *Two women shall be grinding at the mill; the one shall be taken, and the other left.*
>
> **Matthew 24:41**

4. The prodigal son and the elder son:

These two young men lived together in the same house. One was full of rebellion and the other was full of patient obedience. In the end one of these boys became a pauper and the other became a rich man. Originally, they looked like they were both in the perfect will of God. But rebellion destroyed the life of the prodigal son.

> *And he said, A certain man had two sons:*
>
> *And the younger of them said to his father, Father, give me the portion of goods that falleth to me. And he divided unto them his living.*
>
> *And not many days after the younger son gathered all together, and took his journey into a far country, and there wasted his substance with riotous living.*
>
> **Luke 15:11-13**

5. Good salt and salt which has lost its taste:

Good salt and bad salt look exactly the same. There is no way to tell that salt has lost its taste.

The salt of Christians is supposed to make people thirsty for God. Unfortunately, the church has lost much of its flavour and is making people thirst after money and success rather than God.

We have become a wrong kind of salt but we look exactly like good salt. It is not easy to tell when the church is in the imperfect will of God. The salt (gospel ministers) that has lost its flavour is huffing and puffing about grasping worldly things instead of living for God. But it is not easy to see the difference between salt that has lost its flavour and salt that is still salty. Those in the perfect will of God and those in the imperfect will of God look exactly the same.

> *Ye are the salt of the earth: but if the salt have lost his savour, wherewith shall it be salted? It is thenceforth good for nothing, but to be cast out, and to be trodden under foot of men.*
>
> **Matthew 5:13**

6. Good light and bad light:

As the light of the world we are supposed to show the world the path to God, but we rather show them the paths to the world's wealth and glory.

The light that shows the path to God and the light that shows the path to the world are both light and therefore have many similarities. It is difficult to see the difference between these close and parallel lights and yet they point to very different destinations.

> *Ye are the light of the world. A city that is set on an hill cannot be hid. Neither do men light a candle, and put it under a bushel, but on a candlestick; and it giveth light unto all that are in the house.*
>
> *Let your light so shine before men, that they may see your good works, and glorify your father which is in heaven.*
>
> **Matthew 5:14-16**

Chapter 4

The Mysterious Will of God

> *Having made known unto us THE MYSTERY OF HIS WILL, according to his good pleasure which he hath purposed in himself:*
>
> **Ephesians 1:9**

The perfect will of God is mysterious, to say the least. Following the will of God can make you look odd and weird. But you will not shy away from the perfect will of God if you understand that the will of God is essentially mysterious in its nature.

A mysterious thing has strange and often inexplicable features. It is not easily understood and it is often misunderstood. People misunderstand God and often think that He is trying to pull them down or destroy them when He presents His will for their lives.

They cannot fathom this wonderful and mysterious will of the Lord. In this chapter, I want us to look at the many different occasions when the will of God has been mysterious to man. When you understand that the will of God is mysterious, you will not be afraid of it or reject it.

1. The mystery that forsaking Earthly security on God's instructions can give you security.

There are certain things we do to secure our future. Certainly, forsaking your country and your family and launching out into the desert is not one of the ways to secure a great future.

Mysteriously, that was the way Abraham was going to become internationally famous. The mystery of the will of God can be shown in how God gave Abraham a great name on earth with a lasting heritage in Heaven when he walked out into the insecurity and uncertainty of the will of God.

Amazingly, in the story of the Tower of Babel, those who tried to make a great name for themselves amounted to absolutely nothing. Their aims were clearly spelt out. "Let's make a name for ourselves and let's get to Heaven."

> *And they said, go to, let us build us a city and a tower, whose top may reach unto heaven; and let us make us a name, lest we be scattered abroad upon the face of the whole earth.*
>
> **Genesis 11:4**

But they did not accomplish any of these goals.

It is Abraham who mysteriously acquired a great name for himself and got himself into Heaven. How did he do this? "… but the one who does the will of God abides forever" (1 John 2:17, NASB). By simply forsaking the security he had from his country and his family, Abraham embraced the security of walking with God.

> *Now the LORD had said unto Abram, Get thee out of thy country, and from thy kindred, and from thy father's house, unto a land that I will shew thee:*
>
> *And I will make of thee a great nation, and I will bless thee, and MAKE THY NAME GREAT; and thou shalt be a blessing:*
>
> **Genesis 12:1-2**

2. The mystery, that doing nothing, on God's instructions, can give greater results than doing something.

Mysteriously, the perfect will of God can mean that you should stay put and do nothing. It is difficult to do nothing when you are full of life and energy. The mysterious will of God is shown by David's obedience to not build the temple.

By obeying God and doing nothing to build a temple, he allowed his son to build the world-famous Solomon's Temple. Up until today, the building that David did not build forms part of the news and is a major focus of world history. Is it not amazing how great things you can accomplish by doing nothing when God says "do nothing"?

> *And it came to pass the same night, that the word of God came to Nathan, saying, go and tell David my servant, Thus saith the LORD, Thou shalt not build me an house to dwell in:*
>
> **1 Chronicles 17:3-4**

3. The mystery that limiting your ministry to one group of people can cause you to reach all groups of people.

The mysterious will of God is shown by how Jesus reached the whole world by ministering to Jews only. Today Christianity is a non-Jewish religion.

> *And Jesus went away from there, and withdrew into the district of Tyre and Sidon.*
>
> *And behold, a Canaanite woman came out from that region, and began to cry out, saying, "Have mercy on me, O Lord, Son of David; my daughter is cruelly demon-possessed."*
>
> *But He did not answer her a word. And His disciples came to Him and kept asking Him, saying, "Send her away, for she is shouting out after us."*
>
> *But He answered and said, "I WAS SENT ONLY TO THE LOST SHEEP OF THE HOUSE OF ISRAEL."*
>
> **Matthew 15:21-24 (NASB)**

4. The mystery that if it is the will of God you may be more fruitful dead than alive.

The mysterious will of God is shown in Jesus' not travelling all over the world to preach. Rather, by His not continuing to preach but accomplishing His death on the cross, Jesus Christ spread His mission to the whole world.

> *And, behold, there talked with him two men, which were Moses and Elias:*
>
> *Who appeared in glory, and spake of HIS DECEASE WHICH HE SHOULD ACCOMPLISH AT JERUSALEM.*
>
> **Luke 9:30-31**

5. The mystery that losing can lead to gaining.

> *For whosoever will save his life shall lose it: and whosoever will lose his life for my sake shall find it.*
>
> **Matthew 16:25**

Anyone who wants to gain something does everything he can to prevent himself from losing. Yet, here comes Jesus declaring that losing your life is the way to gaining it. How much more mysterious can the will of God be?

6. The mystery that being last can lead to becoming first.

But many that are first shall be last; and the last shall be first.

Matthew 19:30

Is it not mysterious that when you are last you can be first? In every race I know about, it is important to be in the first group or near the front if you are to stand any chance of coming first. Can you imagine your coach telling you, "Be last in this race so you win the medal."

It is not easy to come from behind and pass the people who are far ahead of you. Yet, our Lord says that being last can lead to being first. This is indeed a mystery. How many believe that they will receive the first position by being the last? It is time to stop fighting the mysterious will of God. It is time to embrace it!

7. The mystery that not seeking wealth can make you acquire wealth.

But seek ye first the kingdom of God, and his righteousness; and all these things shall be added unto you."

Matthew 6:33

The mysterious will of God declares that when you seek God you will gain the things you are not pursuing.

Usually, anyone who wants to have a lot of money, food, clothes, must work hard to acquire these things.

Yet Jesus says, "Do not seek them, and do not pursue them and you will get them."

8. The mystery that doing the will of God makes you close to God.

Anyone who does the will of God becomes close to the Lord. I once spoke to a brother who was worried that he would not see me because I was sending him to a far away country.

I said to him, "I have noticed that people who go on the mission field are closer to me than those who stay back home." I often wondered why I became closer to people who were far away. The answer was simple. They were doing what I had asked them to do. You always become closer to somebody who is doing what you want. Jesus said, "For whoever does the will of God, he is My brother and sister and mother!" (Mark 3:35, NASB).

9. The mystery that doing the will of God causes you to make other good decisions for your life.

> *I can of mine own self do nothing: as I hear, I judge: and MY JUDGMENT IS JUST; BECAUSE I SEEK NOT MINE OWN WILL, but the will of the Father which hath sent me.*
>
> **John 5:30**

Jesus said He made good judgment and decisions because He always did the will of the Father. The blessing of being in the perfect will of God is that you make good judgments and decisions.

By following the Lord, you save yourself from many evils that those who are not following His will encounter. Following the Lord into the ministry has forced me to make several good decisions in my personal life.

Chapter 5

Be Filled with the Knowledge of His Will

> *For this reason also, since the day we heard of it, we have not ceased to pray for you and to ask THAT YOU MAY BE FILLED WITH THE KNOWLEDGE OF HIS WILL in all spiritual wisdom and understanding,*
>
> **Colossians 1:9 (NASB)**

When do you need to know the will of God? You must find out the perfect will of God for all important areas of your life. Below is a list of the key areas where you need to know the will of the Lord.

1. **Be filled with the knowledge of His will concerning your calling.**

Will You Function as a Pastor, Prophet, Teacher, Apostle or Evangelist?

Your calling must be according to the will of God. You cannot be a teacher just because you like teaching. You can only be a teacher by the will of God.

You cannot sing just because you like singing. You must sing because it is God's will for your life. You must do only what His will is.

When you start out in ministry, you may have a general kind of calling. But as you mature, your ministry becomes more specific. As you get older, it gets more and more dangerous to stray into areas of ministry God has not called you to. Apostle Paul constantly introduced himself as doing the type of ministry he was doing because of the will of God.

> *Paul, called as an apostle of Jesus Christ by the will of God, and Sosthenes our brother,*
>
> **1 Corinthians 1:1 (NASB)**

> *Paul, an apostle of Jesus Christ by the will of God, and Timothy our brother, unto the church of God which is at Corinth, with all the saints which are in all Achaia:*
>
> **2 Corinthians 1:1**

Paul, an apostle of Jesus Christ by the will of God, to the saints which are at Ephesus, and to the faithful in Christ Jesus:

Ephesians 1:1

Paul, an apostle of Jesus Christ by the will of God, and Timotheus our brother,

Colossians 1:1

Paul, an apostle of Jesus Christ by the will of God, according to the promise of life which is in Christ Jesus...

2 Timothy 1:1

What Is Your Real Calling?

When I started out in ministry, I felt that I was called to be a pastor and a teacher. I always introduced myself as "Pastor and Teacher" Dag Heward-Mills. That was what I understood then. As time went by, I became more and more "filled with the knowledge of His will".

I began to understand that my calling was more of an Apostle and a Teacher than a pastor and a teacher. There is a big difference between the work of a pastor and the work of an apostle.

The apostle has a wider scope of work that involves establishing the churches in different places as against a pastor's work which is caring for and growing one flock of sheep.

When it became clear to me that I was called to be an apostle rather than a pastor, I handed over the church I had pastored for twenty years to a person who had more of the calling of a pastor. I knew that it would be dangerous for me to carry on pastoring that single church.

Every year, as I become more "filled with the knowledge of His will" my understanding of my ministry changes a little. That is how come the roles we play change as the years go by. It is not that we are unstable or uncertain about what God has said but we are gradually being filled with the knowledge of His will and our understanding of how God intends to use us is increasing.

Reversing the Order of Your Call Is Dangerous

Kenneth Hagin, in his book "I Believe in Visions" tells the story of how the Lord appeared to him in hospital, after he had broken his arm in a church service. The Lord told him that he had overheard him telling some pastors how he was called to be first a teacher and then a prophet.

The Lord explained to him that he had opened the door to the devil to attack him because he had reversed the order of his ministry and put the teaching ministry before the prophet's call. Even this was very dangerous and it had opened a door for the enemy to attack him.

Then the Lord warned him that he would not live beyond the age of fifty-five if he continued to reverse the order of his callings.

This is frightening indeed! Not live beyond the age of fifty-five just because you reversed the order of your calling? What then will happen to those who don't even enter their callings in the first place?

You must be filled with the knowledge of His will concerning your calling.

2. Be filled with the knowledge of His will concerning your travels.

All great leaders know that they are more vulnerable when they travel. The perfect will of God is important when a minister is planning his journeys and his ministry. You cannot travel just anywhere you want to. You must go to places God wants you to.

This makes it all the more important to know the will of God when you are planning a journey for the ministry. It is better to stay at home than to go somewhere God has not sent you to.

A quick look at the ministry journeys of most pastors reveals an interesting pattern. Our travels seem to be directed towards wealthy areas and cities. African pastors seem to be mostly "led by the Spirit" to plant churches in European and American destinations.

Similarly, American pastors are mysteriously led to mostly American or European destinations. How come the Holy Spirit is not leading His servants to where most of the souls are?

Could it be that something else is guiding our travels and our journeys? Could money or the lack of it be the real reason for the journeys we make? Or do we make these journeys because they are the will of God?

Dear friend, be careful that every journey you make is by the will of God and not by the will of money!

> *For God, whom I serve in my spirit in the preaching of the gospel of His Son, is my witness as to how unceasingly I make mention of you, always in my prayers making request, IF PERHAPS NOW AT LAST BY THE WILL OF GOD I MAY SUCCEED IN COMING TO YOU.*
>
> **Romans 1:9-10 (NASB)**

> *Now I urge you, brethren, by our Lord Jesus Christ and by the love of the Spirit, to strive together with me in your prayers to God for me, that I may be delivered from those who are disobedient in Judea, and that my service for Jerusalem may prove acceptable to the saints; so that I MAY COME TO YOU IN JOY BY THE WILL OF GOD and find refreshing rest in your company.*
>
> **Romans 15:30-32 (NASB)**

3. Be filled with the knowledge of His will whenever you pray.

The perfect will of God is important when a minister is praying. It is important for a minister to pray only according to the will of God. You cannot just pray about anything you want. You must be led by the Spirit in prayer. You may waste hours praying about things that God will not answer.

Every important person has something that he wants to listen to at a particular time.

God equally has things He wants to hear. When I go to wait on the Lord, I seek to know what He wants me to pray about. One day I came prepared to pray about winning millions of souls in crusades. But I suddenly heard the voice of the Lord, "Pray rather that you may finish your work." I was shocked and a little frightened. My whole prayer time changed and I began to pray about finishing the work God has given me.

It is time to start praying according to the will of God and stop wasting hours on useless gibberish that God is not listening to.

> *And in the same way the Spirit also helps our weakness; for we do not know how to pray as we should, but the Spirit Himself intercedes for us with groanings too deep for words; and He who searches the hearts knows what the mind of the Spirit is, because HE INTERCEDES FOR THE SAINTS ACCORDING TO THE WILL OF GOD.*
>
> **Romans 8:26-27 (NASB)**

4. Be filled with the knowledge of His will concerning your trials and temptations.

The perfect will of God is important when a minister is going through hard times of suffering.

> *Therefore, let THOSE ALSO WHO SUFFER ACCORDING TO THE WILL OF GOD entrust their souls to a faithful Creator in doing what is right.*
> **1 Peter 4:19 (NASB)**

It is important for a minister to suffer only according to the will of God. There are many hard experiences that we go through in the ministry.

You see, there are always two possible reasons for what you are experiencing. You may be in the will of God suffering according to His will that is predetermined. On the other hand you may be suffering from the fruits of your own disobedience.

It is important to seek the will of God about the different suffering experiences God allows you to go through. Why are you suffering? Why are you experiencing what you are experiencing?

Paul Explained His Different Sufferings

All through the New Testament, Paul explained why he went through certain experiences. He would seek the will of God to understand why he was going through the different things he was going through.

When he suffered from a strong demonic battering, he sought the Lord who told him why a thorn in the flesh was given to him to prevent him from becoming proud. The Lord actually explained to him that Satan had been allowed to buffet him for certain mysterious reasons.

> *And lest I should be exalted above measure through the abundance of the revelations, there was given to me a thorn in the flesh, the messenger of Satan to buffet me, lest I should be exalted above measure.*
> **2 Corinthians 12:7**

On another occasion, he explained that he had suffered so much, and had had the sentence of death on his life so that he would not trust in himself at all. "Indeed, we had the sentence of death within ourselves in order that we should not trust in ourselves, but in God who raises the dead;" (2 Corinthians 1:9, NASB).

Yet on another occasion Paul explained that God had spared the life of Epaphroditus because he Paul would not have been able to bear it. "But I thought it necessary to send to you Epaphroditus, my brother and fellow worker and fellow soldier, who is also your messenger and minister to my need; because he was longing for you all was distressed because you had heard that he was sick. For indeed he was sick to the point of death, but God had mercy on him, and not on him only but also on me, lest I should have sorrow upon sorrow" (Philippians 2:25-27, NASB).

Paul also explained that it was because of his apostolic calling that he was experiencing these terrible beatings, shipwrecks, hunger, robbery and imprisonment. He explained that the Lord had set apostles apart for that kind of treatment. "For I think that God hath set forth us the apostles last, as it were appointed to death: for we are made a spectacle unto the world, and to angels, and to men… Even unto this present hour we both hunger, and thirst, and are naked, and are buffeted, and have no certain dwellingplace" (1 Corinthians 4:9, 11).

There are different things that I have experienced in my life and ministry for which I have sought the Lord. I have had difficult experiences in which the Lord showed me why He allowed them.

One day, the Lord told me that He was sorry about the difficulty he had put me through. He added that it was necessary for me to suffer those things.

Do not allow your suffering experiences to pass by without seeking the spiritual explanations and revelations about why they are happening.

5. Be filled with the knowledge of His will concerning your relationships.

> … but they first GAVE THEMSELVES TO THE LORD AND TO US BY THE WILL OF GOD.
>
> **2 Corinthians 8:5 (NASB)**

The perfect will of God is important when you are committing your life to someone. In the ministry, you may have to commit your life to someone who will train, mentor and father you. It is important for you to commit yourself to another human being only according to the will of God.

Years ago, I was reading a book when the Holy Spirit told me to receive the author of the book as a father. That was an important instruction from the Holy Spirit to me. God had decided to use this author and his writings to guide me as a father would personally advise a son.

On several occasions I would open to a page in this man's books and immediately know what I had to do in the ministry. Time and time again, the Lord has spoken clearly to me through this minister's books. It is as though the Holy Spirit spoke audibly to me on different occasions.

You will get closer to the perfect will of God as you openly accept to commit yourself to someone by the will of God.

Following a man and submitting yourself to him is not an easy thing to do. It will be fraught with challenges and tests. If you do not believe that you are in the will of God, your journey of humility and mentorship will end in confusion, accusations and destroyed relationships.

Maintain relationships based on what you believe is the will of God.

6. Be filled with the knowledge of His will concerning your sexual life.

> *For this is the will of God, your sanctification; that is, that you abstain from sexual immorality; that each of*

> *you know how to possess his own vessel in sanctification and honor,*
>
> **1 Thessalonians 4:3-4 (NASB)**

The perfect will of God is for a minister to abstain from sexual immorality. The will of God is clear about fornication. Since that is one of the clearest directions of the Lord it is important that you make it one of your clearest and most energetic goals to practically live a sexually pure life. Stay away from anyone who would want to have such a relationship with you.

Everyone has a different way by which he keeps himself from fornication.

You must find out what is God's will for your life's journey of staying away from fornication. It may be God's will for you to never read certain books or watch certain films and that may be the way you will stay away from fornication.

It may be God's will for you to marry as a very young man in order to keep yourself from fornication. It may be God's will for you to have sex with your spouse every day in order to keep you from fornication. It may be the will of God for you to never live in certain countries that are more immoral.

It may be God's will for you to travel everywhere with your wife in order to stay away from fornication. It may be the will of God for you not to have certain friends in order to avoid fornication.

It may be God's will for you never to work with women or have female secretaries in order to keep you from fornication.

What is the will of God for your specific circumstance and situation? When it comes to possessing your vessel in sanctification, everyone should know how it works best for him and what the will of the Lord is.

> *For this is the will of God, even your sanctification, that ye should abstain from fornication:*
>
> **1 Thessalonians 4:3**

7. Be filled with the knowledge of His will concerning church growth.

> *And this is the Father's will which hath sent me, that of all which he hath given me I should lose nothing, but should raise it up again at the last day.*
>
> **John 6:39**

The perfect will of God is for a minister not to lose any of the members that God has given him. If you are a pastor and you want to know the will of God, look no further, you have found the Scripture you need. It is the will of God that you lose none of the sheep that He has given to you. Keep fighting to grow your church.

Church growth is the will of God. Fight to keep every single person God draws to your ministry. Fight to have a mega church. Teach about commitment and devotion. Do everything you can, so that you do not lose any of your members. That is the will of God for you. It is the will of God for you to fight wolves who come to eat your sheep. Don't feel bad because you are in conflict with people who try to destroy the church. If you have a lame response to rebels and disloyal elements in your churches, you will not be able to say, "Of all that you have given me I have lost nothing."

8. Be filled with the knowledge of His will concerning finishing your work on earth.

The perfect will of God is for a minister is to finish the work he has been given on the earth. God's will is that you should finish the work He has given you.

Your death comes shortly after you finish your work. You remain on this earth only because of unfinished work that has been assigned to you.

One day, whilst waiting on the Lord I heard Him say to me, "Pray that you may finish your work." I was shaken and I knew that it was a very important spiritual goal that I finish the work He has given to me. This is the will of God for you: that you finish the work He has given to you. Have you finished your work in your country? Have you finished your work in your church? Have you finished your work in the lives of your disciples? Make sure you finish the work you have been given to do.

One day, I realised that I had trained my disciples to do many things but I had not trained them to build buildings and to do administrative work. I had done all the building and administrative work myself. I realised that they did not even understand how the church functioned administratively.

Suddenly I knew that I had not finished my work of training them. I decided to stop building things and to stop doing administrative things so that they would have the opportunity to learn this hidden, but important, aspect of the ministry.

> *Jesus saith unto them, My meat is to do the will of him that sent me, and to finish his work.*
>
> **John 4:34**

9. Be filled with the knowledge of His will concerning your personal ambitions.

> *For I came down from heaven, not to do mine own will, but the will of him that sent me.*
>
> **John 6:38**

> *I can of mine own self do nothing: as I hear, I judge: and my judgment is just; because I seek not mine own will, but the will of the Father which hath sent me.*
>
> **John 5:30**

The perfect will of God for a minister is not to pursue his own will but to do the will of God who sent him.

It is important to MAKE IT YOUR DESIRE NOT TO DO YOUR OWN WILL but the will of the Father.

A minister who will succeed is someone who will constantly PUT ASIDE HIS OWN WILL and submit to the will of the Father. We all have childhood dreams and personal human ambitions. But none of these must interfere with God's will for your life and ministry.

Perhaps, as a child, you desired to live in America. But the will of the Lord may be that you live and minister in Africa. If a door therefore opens for you to live in America, you must set aside your own will and do the will of God.

Chapter 6

Twenty Reasons Why You Must Be Led by the Spirit of God

... if thou shalt hearken... God will set thee on high...
Deuteronomy 28:1

1. You must be led by the Spirit of God so that the Lord can lift you high above your colleagues and contemporaries.

Israel had just become a nation and needed to grow and prosper like every nation does. The newly born nation of Israel was surrounded by other nations with similar aspirations. The Lord gave them the key that would set them above all the nations around.

> *If you will LISTEN DILIGENTLY TO THE VOICE of the Lord your God, being watchful to do all His commandments which I command you this day, the Lord your God will set you high above all the nations of the earth.*
>
> **Deuteronomy 28: 1 (AMP)**

Deuteronomy 28:1 teaches that hearkening or listening to the voice of God is the key to promotion above your contemporaries and colleagues.

Listening to the voice of God will set you above others in the same class. This is one of the foremost reasons why you must be led by the Spirit of God.

Many years ago, I heard Kenneth Hagin say that the difference between ministers is their ability to be led by the Spirit of God.

Kenneth Hagin also spoke about how the Lord told him that He would make him rich if he were led by the Spirit. I believe this too. Anyone who follows the voice of God will experience great prosperity.

The ability to hear the voice of the Lord and to follow him is the key factor that differentiates ministers of the gospel. You go up or down based on this *ability*. That is why it is so crucial for every pastor and minister to wait on God and to learn how to be led by the Spirit of God. You must learn how to be led by the Spirit of God into the perfect will of God.

In the perfect will of God you will find all your needs met and all your prayers answered. In the perfect will of God you will fit appropriately into God's plan for your life. In the perfect will of God you will attain to all the spiritual heights that God has destined for you and your calling.

Every minister of the gospel must develop himself in the art of hearing God's voice. What does God's voice sound like? What are the different ways by which God speaks? What are the mistakes one can make when trying to follow the voice of God?

Since this is what will make the big difference in your life and ministry, why would you not give the greatest attention to this all-important "art of hearing" God's voice? It is sad that many ministers do not give time and attention to the art of hearing the voice of God.

2. You must be led by the Spirit of God so that you will be in the perfect will of God.

Following the Spirit of God into the perfect will of God must be your aim. Does He speak through books?

Does He speak through pastors?

Does He speak through an inner voice?

Does He speak when I fast?

If you do not succeed in this quest for hearing the voice of God, your ministry will not amount to much. You must seek to find what is that good and acceptable and perfect will of God (Romans 12:2).

Any kind of ministry that is not done in the perfect will of God will not amount to much.

3. You must be led by the Spirit of God so that you will avoid the imperfect will of God and its consequences.

> *And the LORD opened the mouth of the ass, and she said unto Balaam, What have I done unto thee, that thou hast smitten me these three times?*
>
> *And Balaam said unto the ass, Because thou hast mocked me: I would there were a sword in mine hand, for now would I kill thee.*
>
> *And the ass said unto Balaam, AM NOT I THINE ASS, UPON WHICH THOU HAST RIDDEN EVER SINCE I WAS THINE UNTO THIS DAY? WAS I EVER WONT TO DO SO UNTO THEE? And he said, Nay.*
>
> *Then the LORD opened the eyes of Balaam, and he saw the angel of the LORD standing in the way, and his sword drawn in his hand: and he bowed down his head, and fell flat on his face.*
>
> **Numbers 22:28-31**

When you go into the imperfect will of God, forces will be released to oppose your mission. Balaam found his own donkey turning against him. The donkey that had served him well for many years turned against him. The things that had worked for him for many years no longer worked.

An angel with a sword was sent from Heaven to destroy him. Why? Because he had gone out of the perfect will of God and prophesied on issues that did not please the Lord.

You must only go on missions that God has sent you to. You must always be in His perfect will and not what He is just allowing. Failure to understand or to perceive God's will is a dangerous thing for a minister of the gospel.

4. You must be led by the Spirit of God so that you avoid error.

> ... YE DO ERR, not knowing the SCRIPTURES, nor the POWER of God.
>
> **Matthew 22:29**

There are two types of ministers: those who love dreams, visions and prophetic things. The other type are those who love the solid Word of God.

People who base their lives *only* on the written Word easily go into error.

On the other hand, those who live their lives mainly by following visions and prophecies are equally prone to error.

Error comes when you are *only* guided by the written Word of God.

Error comes when you are bereft of dreams and visions and prophecies! Error comes when you only live by the rules and principles of the Word of God but deny the leading of the Holy Spirit. Do you want to be in error? Do you want to deviate from the will of God? Of course not! You must believe in the Bible but you must be led by the Spirit of God.

5. You must be led by the Spirit of God so that you avoid the futility of your mind.

> *This I say therefore, and affirm together with the Lord, that you walk NO LONGER JUST AS THE GENTILES ALSO WALK, IN THE FUTILITY OF THEIR MIND, being darkened in their understanding, excluded from the life of God, because of the ignorance that is in them, because of the hardness of their heart;*
>
> **Ephesians 4:17-18 (NASB)**

Christians must forsake the world and the lifestyle of the unbeliever. The lifestyle of the unbeliever is characterized by walking in the "futility of the mind". The mind is a gift from God. But the mind on its own leads many astray into darkness and futility.

If you want a good example of what it is like to walk in the futility of the mind, take a look at Europe. With their minds they have developed perfection in areas such as finance, development, health, education, etc. As they continued to walk in the light of their human minds, they progressed into atheism, homosexuality and many other perversions.

The Scripture is clear in its warnings about walking in the "futility of the mind". This is where the Holy Spirit comes in, guiding us step by step, often contrary to natural thinking.

It is even more tragic when ministers of the gospel walk in the "futility of their mind"; having not the Spirit and His greatly needed influence.

The voice of God is important for every area of your life. Open up every area of your life to the direction of God's Spirit.

You may think that God is not interested in certain areas of your life. God has something to say about every aspect of your life. The Lord is depicted as a shepherd to His sheep. Sheep are animals that are greatly dependent on human beings for everything. If the Lord is your Shepherd then following him will cause you not to want or need any good thing.

6. You must be led by the Spirit of God so that all your needs are met.

The LORD is my shepherd; I shall not want.

Psalm 23:1

The first sign that you are being led by the voice of the Holy Spirit is "not wanting". "I shall not want" is what you will say after you have followed the Shepherd for some time! You will be able to say with David, "I have no needs; I am blessed in every way." In order to experience this, you must follow the leading of the Spirit.

Don't you want to experience the abundance of all things? Be led by the Spirit of God and you will never lack any good thing.

7. You must be led by the Spirit of God so that you live in fresh and restful places.

The sign that you are being led by the voice of the Holy Spirit is a peaceful home and resting place. You must follow the Holy Spirit until He gives you a restful marriage and home. Without the guidance of the Holy Spirit into the perfect will of God, you will never lie down in peaceful green pastures.

> *He maketh me to lie down in green pastures: he leadeth me beside the still waters.*
>
> **Psalm 23:2**

Green pasture speaks of peace and happiness. It speaks of the marriages we all desire.

You will never have true happiness unless you marry the person God wants you to marry. If you allow Him, the Holy Spirit will lead you to a peaceful marriage.

8. You must be led by the Spirit of God so that you live a righteous life.

A sign that you are being led by the voice of the Holy Spirit is that you end up living a righteous life. You must follow the Holy Spirit until He leads you into righteousness. Depend on the voice of God for the *right church*, the *right friends* and the *right company*.

> *He restoreth my soul: he leadeth me in the paths of righteousness for his name's sake.*
>
> **Psalm 23:3**

This Scripture shows how dependent you are on God's guidance for righteous living.

Many people end up as fruitless nonentities in the kingdom of God because they do not follow the leading of the Spirit into the perfect will of God.

Many people join churches just because they live near the church. Others join churches because the pastor is handsome or because they like the pastor's wife. But it is so important to be led by the Spirit when you are choosing a church.

It makes all the difference in the world! Most definitely, you need the guidance of the Holy Spirit to know where to go to church.

9. You must be led by the Spirit of God so that you will not be afraid of death.

A sign that you are being led by the voice of the Holy Spirit is fearlessness. You must follow the Holy Spirit until He gives you a life without tears. Depend on the voice of God for *divine protection*.

> *Yea, though I walk through the valley of the shadow of death, I will fear no evil: for thou art with me; thy rod and thy staff they comfort me.*
>
> **Psalm 23:4**

The psalmist made it clear that he was dependent on the Shepherd for protection. He explained how the Lord's protection was so powerful that he was able to eat lunch when his enemy was nearby.

Listening to the news, it is almost as though travellers are playing Russian roulette. Russian roulette is a game involving the firing of a revolver that has only one out of the six chambers loaded. Each time you point the gun at your head and fire, you have one out of the six chances of dying.

If you are the unlucky one, the bullet will be fired when you pull the trigger. Sometimes, it looks as though your life is a game of chance. Definitely, you need the voice of God to choose the right car, bus, plane or train!

When you follow the Spirit into the perfect will of God you can rest assured that you will live as long as God wants you to and die on the day that God has ordained.

10. You must be led by the Spirit of God so that you become anointed.

As you are led by the Spirit of God you will be filled by the Holy Spirit and the anointing. You must follow the Holy Spirit until He fills you. Depend on the voice of God for *the Anointing*.

> *... thou anointest my head with oil; my cup runneth over.*
>
> **Psalm 23:5**

Without being directed by the Lord, you will never be anointed. The anointing will not come from Heaven per se.

All anointed men caught the anointing by relating with certain people on earth. God will have to direct you to relate with anointed men of God. Jesus told His disciples, "Follow me and I will make you…" Without following the right person, you will not amount to much in the ministry.

Surely, God will lead you to the right person by the Holy Spirit.

11. You must be led by the Spirit of God so that you enjoy the good things in this life.

> *Surely goodness and mercy shall follow me all the days of my life…*
>
> **Psalm 23:6**

The silver and the gold belong to the Lord. If you seek His face, He will show you where it is hidden! "The silver is mine, and the gold is mine, saith the LORD of hosts" (Haggai 2:8).

As you are led by the Spirit of God, expect to find the silver and gold on this earth.

You will experience goodness and mercies by following the Holy Spirit. You must follow the Holy Spirit until He gives you goodness and mercies. Every businessman must know the voice of the Holy Spirit. Without the help of God you will never make it to the top.

12. You must be led by the voice of God so that you eventually go to Heaven.

As you follow the Holy Spirit you will make it to the streets of gold. If you follow the Holy Spirit throughout your life on earth you will receive eternal crowns in glory.

> ... and I will dwell in the house of the Lord for ever.
> **Psalm 23:6**

Do you want to dwell in the house of the Lord forever? As you follow the Spirit of God, He will lead you on the path of righteousness. This will eventually lead to Heaven. You need the Shepherd to take you from the green pastures to the streets of gold.

13. You must be led by the Spirit of God to avoid getting into big trouble.

Studying the voice of God can be a little frightening, especially when you think of the consequences that can befall you when you do not obey His voice. Years ago I noticed this Scripture,

> *For though I preach the gospel, I have nothing to glory of: for necessity is laid upon me; yea, WOE IS UNTO ME, IF I PREACH NOT THE GOSPEL!*
>
> **1 Corinthians 9:16**

Paul was someone who felt he would get into all sorts of trouble if he did not preach the Gospel. He was not wrong!

Indeed, I think I can say with Paul, "Woe is unto me, if I preach not the Gospel."

Every minister who does not take the leading of the Spirit seriously will open himself to all sorts of dangerous attacks. He will be in danger of losing the anointing!

Woe to the people who do not spend their lives preaching when God has called them to preach.

14. You must be led by the Spirit of God to avoid losing your gift.

> *And he said unto them that stood by, Take from him the pound, and give it to him that hath ten pounds.*
>
> **Luke 19:24**

Dear man of God, do not think that you are indispensable. If you do not do what God wants you to do, your ministry will be taken away from you and given to another.

Read it for yourself!

Take from him the pound!

Give it to somebody else!

If God gave you a pound, He can take it back when He wants to. We the ministers of the gospel love to hide behind Romans 11:29.

> *For the gifts and calling of God are without repentance.*
>
> **Romans 11:29**

Because of this verse, we think that God will never take away His anointing. But that cannot be the case. What this Scripture means is that God does not change His mind about you. He never changes His decision to call you or use you. **He never changes His decision to anoint you.**

If God has called you to be a vessel, you will always be a vessel. The story of the Prophet Jonah is a good example of how God does not change His mind about the people He wants to use. Jonah did not want to go where the Lord had sent him. He wanted to be a nice guy everybody liked.

> *Now the word of the LORD came unto Jonah the son of Amittai, saying, Arise, go to Nineveh, that great city, and cry against it; for their wickedness is come up before me. But Jonah rose up to flee unto Tarshish from the presence of the LORD, and went down to Joppa; and he found a ship going to Tarshish: so he paid the fare thereof, and went down into it, to go with*

them unto Tarshish from the presence of the LORD. But the LORD sent out a great wind into the sea, and there was a mighty tempest in the sea, so that the ship was like to be broken.

Jonah 1:1-4

However, when the season of grace is over, God will have no choice but to recall His pound. He may have to give this pound to another more faithful minister.

Will You Write This Book?

I remember a man of God whom the Lord spoke to about writing a book. The Lord asked him, "Will you write this book?"

He said, "Yes Lord, of course I will!"

And the Lord said, "I hope so, because you are the fifth person I have asked to write this book. If you do not write it, I will move on to the sixth person."

Dear friend, in this story you see two principles working together. On one hand, God does not change His mind about writing the book. On the other, God is forced to select someone else and give him the job.

Yes, I believe that God does not change His mind about us. But I also know that God can recall His pound and give it to another.

> *And he said unto them that stood by, TAKE FROM HIM THE POUND, and give it to him that hath ten pounds.*
>
> **Luke 19:24**

Keep the gift of God by obeying His call! Be sensitive to His voice! Do what He tells you to do and you will succeed in ministry! Do what is hard and difficult rather than what is nice and easy!

> *And cast ye the unprofitable servant into outer darkness: there shall be weeping and gnashing of teeth.*
>
> **Matthew 25:30**

The expression "weeping and gnashing of teeth" is a little misunderstood by most of us. We often think it refers to Hell and Hades. However, the Bible does not explicitly say that the people will go to Hell. It says that they will weep and gnash their teeth in darkness. Weeping speaks of the sorrow and pain associated with death.

This Scripture could be warning the servants of God that failure to obey could cost them their very lives.

15. You must be led by the Spirit of God to avoid premature death.

Kenneth Hagin, a great prophet I deeply respect, often spoke of how ministers died before their time because they did not obey the Lord concerning their ministry. He spoke of how he broke his arm and was admitted to the hospital. When the Lord Jesus appeared to him in the hospital, he discovered that his accident had occurred because he did not take an aspect of his ministry seriously.

Dear friend, doing the work of God is not a joke. It is not a game! People were made to experience weeping and gnashing of teeth because they were unprofitable. "Unprofitable" simply means *"unbeneficial, running at a loss, unsuccessful and losing money (souls)"*.

When you are losing souls for the Lord, do not expect Him to be pleased with you. He may have to recall or replace you.

The Picture

I remember a testimony given by the pastor of one of the world's largest churches. He described how he was rummaging through some old pictures. He noticed a picture that was taken during his Bible school days. There were about fifty people in his graduating class. As he mused over the picture, he realized that forty-five of his classmates were dead.

He then remembered that the five who were still alive, were the only ones who were serious about prayer during their Bible school days. He also realized that they were the only ones who took the ministry seriously after Bible school. Many of the others had become welders, carpenters, lawyers, etc. and they were all dead.

Dear friend, the call of God is serious business. God does not take lightly the investment that He has placed in you. To whom much is given, much is required!

> *... For unto whomsoever much is given, of him shall be much required...*
>
> **Luke 12:48**

If you desert the army during wartime, your punishment is often execution. Everyone who withholds his gifts and abilities in a time of war is cursed.

> *Cursed be he that doeth the work of the LORD deceitfully, and cursed be he that keepeth back his sword from blood.*
>
> **Jeremiah 48:10**

Those Who Obey and Disobey

> *And, behold, there came a man of God out of Judah by the word of the LORD unto Bethel: and Jeroboam stood by the altar to burn incense. And he cried against the altar in the word of the LORD, and said, O altar, altar, thus saith the LORD; Behold, a child shall be born unto the house of David, Josiah by name; and upon thee shall he offer the priests of the high places that burn incense upon thee, and men's bones shall be burnt upon thee. And he gave a sign the same day, saying, This is the sign which the LORD hath spoken; Behold, the altar shall be rent, and the ashes that are upon it shall be poured out.*

And it came to pass, when king Jeroboam heard the saying of the man of God, which had cried against the altar in Bethel, that he put forth his hand from the altar, saying, Lay hold on him. And his hand, which he put forth against him, dried up, so that he could not pull it in again to him. The altar also was rent, and the ashes poured out from the altar, according to the sign which the man of God had given by the word of the LORD.

And the king answered and said unto the man of God, Intreat now the face of the LORD thy God, and pray for me, that my hand may be restored me again. And the man of God besought the LORD, and the king's hand was restored him again, and became as it was before. And the king said unto the man of God, Come home with me, and refresh thyself, and I will give thee a reward.

And the man of God said unto the king, if thou wilt give me half thine house, I will not go in with thee, neither will I eat bread nor drink water in this place: For so was it charged me by the word of the LORD, saying, Eat no bread, nor drink water, nor turn again by the same way that thou camest. So he went another way, and returned not by the way that he came to Bethel.

Now there dwelt an old prophet in Bethel; and his sons came and told him all the works that the man of God had done that day in Bethel: the words which he had spoken unto the king, them they told also to their father. And their father said unto them, What way went he? For his sons had seen what way the man of God went, which came from Judah. And he said unto his sons, Saddle me the ass. So they saddled him the ass: and he rode thereon; And went after the man of God, and found him sitting under an oak: and he said unto him, Art thou the man of God that camest from Judah? And he said, I am. Then he said unto him, Come home with me, and eat bread. And he said, I may not return with thee, nor go in with thee: neither will I eat bread or drink water with thee in this place: For it was said to me by the word of the LORD, Thou shalt eat no bread nor drink water there, nor turn again to go by the way that thou camest.

He said unto him, I am a prophet also as thou art; and an angel spake unto me by the word of the LORD, saying, Bring him back with thee into thine house, that he may eat bread and drink water. But he lied unto him. So he went back with him, and did eat bread in his house, and drank water.

And it came to pass, as they sat at the table, that the word of the Lord came unto the prophet that brought him back: And he cried unto the man of God that came from Judah, saying, Thus saith the LORD, Forasmuch as thou hast disobeyed the mouth of the LORD, and hast not kept the commandment which the LORD thy God commanded thee, But camest back, and hast eaten bread and drunk water in the place, of the which the LORD did say to thee, Eat no bread, and drink no water; thy carcase shall not come unto the sepulchre of thy fathers.

And it came to pass, after he had eaten bread, and after he had drunk, that he saddled for him the ass, to wit, for the prophet whom he had brought back. And when he was gone, a lion met him by the way, and

> slew him: and his carcase was cast in the way, and the ass stood by it, the lion also stood by the carcase. And, behold, men passed by, and saw the carcase cast in the way, and the lion standing by the carcase: and they came and told it in the city where the old prophet dwelt.
>
> And when the prophet that brought him back from the way heard thereof, he said, It is the man of God, who was disobedient unto the word of the LORD: therefore the LORD hath delivered him unto the lion, which hath torn him, and slain him, according to the word of the LORD, which he spake unto him.
>
> **1 Kings 13:1-26**

In this story, the Lord specifically told the prophet what to do. By obeying the voice of God this man of God became a worker of signs and wonders. He suddenly had a thriving ministry.

Then here comes an old and backslidden man of God. Did you know that men of God could also backslide? Unfortunately, this younger prophet listened to another "voice".

At a certain level of ministry, you may become confused by the different voices that are trying to guide you. Make sure that you stick with the Word of God.

In the New Testament, Paul explicitly stated that people were sick and dead because they did not discern the Lord's Body.

Paul gave the reason for disease and death in the church.

> *For he that eateth and drinketh unworthily, eateth and drinketh damnation to himself, not discerning the Lord's body. For this cause many are weak and sickly among you, and many sleep [dead].*
>
> **1 Corinthians 11:29, 30**

To discern the Lord's Body means to realize or discern that you are dealing with the Lord's Body. All the sheep and little lambs are the Lord's Body. They are the ones He died for on the cross.

If for instance, you knew that somebody's finger was on the table, you would not strike it with a big hammer. You would not hit that finger because you know it is part of his body.

When you fail to realize that the church is Christ's Body, you will get into trouble. Those sheep, those people, are the ones the Lord shed His blood for! They are His body! When you abandon them, it is like abandoning your mouth (a part of your body) by not brushing your teeth for months. You can imagine why the Lord gets mad at ministers who neglect His Body.

16. You must be led by the Spirit of God to avoid being replaced.

Jesus died for the little lambs. He told us to "go!" He told us to feed His little lambs. One day, the Lord became very angry with His shepherds. Look at what He said to them. He said He would take over and shepherd the people Himself.

> *Therefore, ye shepherds, hear the word of the LORD; As I live, saith the Lord GOD, surely because my flock became a prey, and my flock became meat to every beast of the field, because there was no shepherd, neither did my shepherds search for my flock, but the shepherds fed themselves, and fed not my flock; Thus saith the Lord GOD; Behold, I am against the shepherds; and I will require my flock at their hand, and cause them to cease from feeding the flock; neither shall the shepherds feed themselves any more; for I will deliver my flock from their mouth, that they may not be meat for them. FOR THUS SAITH THE LORD GOD; BEHOLD, I, EVEN I, WILL BOTH SEARCH MY SHEEP, AND SEEK THEM OUT.*
>
> **Ezekiel 34:7, 8, 10, 11**

One night, while in a hotel in South America, the Lord spoke to me about His work. I had never heard the Lord speak as mournfully as He did that night. He spoke of how nobody cared about His work. He told me that everyone was running about his or her own business. He said to me, "No one cares about my work." I found this very sad but real.

When we do not obey the Lord, we are in effect neglecting His sheep. Jesus asked Peter whether he would feed the sheep. Peter was taken aback, wondering why the Lord was asking. "After three years of training what do you expect me to do?" he must have thought. But the Lord knows how many ministers abandon His work for other pursuits!

When a minister neglects or abandons God's work, the Lord gets angry. This is the reason why He often displaces and replaces men of God with new ones.

A Vision of Replacement

One day I had a strange vision. In this vision, I saw a man being lifted from his chair by the collar of his neck. I did not see who the man was. Suddenly, I found myself being lifted by the collar of my neck and being placed in his chair.

After that the Lord told me that I was replacing someone in the ministry.

Dear friend, I tell you, I was frightened! I was not frightened about replacing someone. Rather I was worried that I could be replaced by someone else one day. This vision is biblical because it has happened many times in the Scriptures.

Samuel replaced Eli! David replaced Saul! Elisha replaced Elijah! Joshua replaced Moses! Esther replaced Vashti!

> *... and Elisha the son of Shaphat of Abel-meholah shalt thou anoint to be prophet in thy room.*
> **1 Kings 19:16**

You have a room (place) in the ministry. However, it is not a permanent room. It can be given to anyone who deserves it. Always remember that there are people ready to replace you if you do not obey the voice of God. Obey the voice of God to avoid replacement!

17. You must be led by the Spirit of God so that you abide in the presence of God.

The voice of the Lord is one of the cardinal signs of His presence. Think about it! When someone is present in a home, you hear his voice. When a person dies and is no longer around, you no longer hear his voice because he is no longer present.

You will notice that ministers who hear from God have a certain aura and presence around them. This is because they are near enough to His presence and are hearing His voice.

This is an important revelation because it helps you not to depend on things which are not sure signs of His presence.

Success and wealth are not signs of God's presence. It is true that the presence of a person may mean that the fridge will be full of food.

But suffering and sad experiences do not mean that God is not with you. Paul had many difficult experiences but he said that none of those things could separate him from the love of God.

A sure sign of the presence of God and the anointing is His voice. Seek for His voice everyday. Do not allow His voice to grow dim and faint.

18. You must be led by the Spirit of God so that you do not grieve Him.

And grieve not the Holy Spirit of God, whereby ye are sealed unto the day of redemption.

Ephesians 4:30

Following the Holy Spirit is important so that you do not grieve Him. If the Holy Spirit tries to lead you and you shut Him out, He will be grieved. Someone who is often quieted down at meetings becomes grieved. Someone who is often ignored becomes grieved and does not give of his best.

When you shut out the voice of the Holy Spirit, He is grieved and does not give you His input anymore. You may have the Holy Spirit but He will be grieving and inactive in your life.

19. You must be led by the Spirit of God so that you do not quench Him.

Do not quench (suppress or subdue) the [Holy] Spirit

1 Thessalonians 5:19 (AMP)

As you continue to ignore the Holy Spirit you will eventually put out His voice from your life. This is more serious than grieving Him. Grieving speaks of a pause in the Holy Spirit's input but quenching speaks of putting a fire out. When a fire is quenched it is put out permanently.

The Holy Spirit's input in your life can be permanently wiped out. Do not permanently silence the Holy Spirit in your life.

20. You must be led by the Spirit of God so that you do not anger Him.

> *Think how much more terrible the punishment will be for those who have trampled on the Son of God and have treated the blood of the covenant as if it were common and unholy. SUCH PEOPLE HAVE INSULTED AND ENRAGED THE HOLY SPIRIT who brings God's mercy to his people.*
>
> **Hebrews 10:29 (NLT)**

After grieving or quenching the Holy Spirit, you can enter into a very dangerous dimension in relation to the wonderful Holy Spirit who has been given to guide you in this life. You can insult him and anger Him.

Taking someone for granted and acting presumptuously can be insulting.

Years of being ignored, being quenched and being set aside can amount to deep insult to the Spirit of Grace. You must obey the voice of the Spirit so that you do not become guilty of insulting the mighty Holy Spirit.

Chapter 7

Twelve Different Kinds of Voices

There are, it may be, so many kinds of voices in the world, and none of them is without signification.

1 Corinthians 14:10

One of the greatest desires of all serious Christians is to know the will of God. With a little experience in life, anyone can tell that there are many different ways your life can go. We often come to the crossroads and ask, "Which way is best?" If you take the wrong road, the implications may be devastating. If you marry the wrong person, the consequences may be terrible. If you join the wrong church, the consequences may be eternal.

Many times when we take decisions, we are unable to retrace our steps. In other words, many decisions are irreversible. Because of this, we need to know the will of God so that we can be guided along every step of the way.

Even Unbelievers Want to Know the Future

Unbelievers have ways of getting to know what is best for them. Many of them consult soothsayers, astrologers and fortune tellers. They put their trust in false prophets and occult power. They also see the need to know what to do next. African politicians are often said to consult these powers on a regular basis. They often ask for direction and protection from them. African soccer teams are also said to consult these mediums. You will notice however, that none of these things have taken them very far.

As Christians, we do not need to consult satanic powers to know the future. God has graciously given us the Holy Spirit to guide us. Being led by the Spirit of God is a sign that you are a true Christian.

> *For as many as are led by the Spirit of God, they are the sons of God.*
>
> **Romans 8:14**

In the Old Testament, only the prophet seemed to know the will of God. You see, the Holy Spirit was not given to everyone at that time. We are living in a blessed dispensation. We all have the Holy Spirit in us and can be led by the Spirit of God. It is possible for us to know the will of God. That is what this book is all about:

"How to know the will of God" and "How to be led by the Spirit of God."

Twelve Different Kinds of Voices

The first step to knowing the will of God is to recognize that there are many types of voices in this world and all of them are trying to influence you. The art of selecting the right voice and listening to that voice is the art of being led by the Spirit of God.

God wants to deliver you from evil and He has sent His Spirit to lead you through this life so that you will not make tragic mistakes. Satan, who is God's opponent and an opposition party, is trying to lead you in the wrong way or at least confuse you. What are the voices that are trying to influence you? There are several possibilities that you must be aware of:

1. The voice of God

2. The voice of the flesh

3. The voice of the mind

4. The voice of the devil

5. The voice of a prophet

6. The voice of the Bible

7. The voice of your friends

8. The voice of your parents

9. The voice of your spirit

10. The voice of your spouse

11. The voice of circumstances

12. The voice of your own will.

All these voices, as well as some others, are probably in operation in your life. Depending on who you are, you may be influenced more or less by these voices. A young man may claim that the voice of God spoke to him, directing him to marry a beautiful young lady in the church. He may approach the young woman and tell her, "God spoke to me last night." Is this young man telling the truth? Did he really hear the voice of God?

Let me make an important point here. There are at least twelve different voices that this young man could have heard. He could have heard the voice of circumstances leading him to marry this young lady or he could have heard the voice of his flesh, desirous of the opposite sex. He could also have genuinely heard the voice of God. None of these voices is without significance. What is important is to know which voice is leading you.

The Thirsty Donkey

I always remember the story of a thirsty donkey that went on a long journey through the desert. At the end of his tedious journey, the donkey was tired, hungry and thirsty. As it trudged along, it noticed two stacks of hay at different ends of the field. The donkey thought to himself, "There is food for me!" Then he realized that the two different haystacks were at opposite ends of an extremely large field.

The donkey, being a "Christian", decided to seek the will of God concerning which of the haystacks he should approach. The donkey decided to pray. As the donkey was bowing his head to pray, he noticed a bucket of water positioned by the haystack on the right. The donkey then prayed a simple but powerful prayer and said, "O God, I want to know your will concerning which direction to go. Should I go to the haystack on the right or to the one on the left?"

After praying, the donkey gathered himself together and began to walk towards one of the haystacks. Which of the stacks of hay do you think the donkey went to? The stack on the right or that on the left? Well, when the donkey was asked he said, "God has directed me to the one on the right."

Everyone can predict that the donkey would say that God had directed him to the haystack on the right. However, you and I both know that it was probably the bucket of water that attracted the donkey to the haystack on the right. It is time to be honest! It is time to tell the truth! Is it really the Spirit of God who is leading us or is it the voice of our flesh and of circumstances?

Anytime someone claims to have been directed by the "Spirit of God", you should remember that there are over twelve different possibilities that exist. The voice he claims to be hearing is one out of twelve or more different voices. Is it the voice of his friends? Is it the voice of his wife? Is it the voice of circumstances? What is actually leading this person?

Three in One Day!

I learnt of a man who became close to three Christian sisters at the same time. This man happened to be in Bible school at the same time with these three ladies who were his age. They attended classes together, they prayed together and they even went to church together. As time passed, they became a very closely knit family. There was a real flow of Christian love and friendship among them. This Christian brother was a very caring young man. He was also handsome and was obviously a promising minister. He was good at the ministry of counselling and seemed to be a patient listener to people's problems.

At the end of the course, something interesting happened! It was graduation time and each of the three Christian sisters approached this compassionate brother with a "message" from the Lord. Each one of them said (unknown to the others), "God has spoken to me about you that we should spend the rest of our lives and ministries together." In other words, God had supposedly spoken to each of these women to marry the brother. The brother was so surprised. He told them, "I appreciate your sharing this with me, but God hasn't spoken to me about this." He did not marry any of these three girls. He ended up marrying somebody else.

I find this true story very interesting. It illustrates the point I am trying to make. Each of these three ladies claimed to have heard the voice of God. But as I said, there are several possibilities to each claim. How could God tell three different people, at the same time, to marry one man? Does His Word not tell us that God wants one man to marry only one woman?

They were obviously hearing the voice of their own flesh. It could be the voice of their minds. They claimed that the voice of their flesh was the voice of God. These three ladies embarrassed themselves. You can save yourself from embarrassment when you learn to distinguish between the voice of the Spirit and other voices. That is what this book is all about – how to know the voice of God and how to follow the Holy Spirit to the top! In the following chapters, I will share some things about these different voices and how you can distinguish between them.

Four Things Every Christian Should Know about the Voice of the Mind

And the very God of peace sanctify you wholly; and I pray God your whole SPIRIT and SOUL and BODY be preserved blameless unto the coming of our Lord Jesus Christ.

1 Thessalonians 5:23

Man consists of a spirit, a soul and a body. That is quite clear from the verse above. Each of these components of the human being has a voice.

Your thought processes and your reasoning are the voice of your mind. God never intended for us to do away with our minds. Many people stop reasoning and thinking when they become Christians. There is a funny notion that it is wrong to reason or understand things once you are in the kingdom of God. There is a feeling that if you are a spiritual person it is not right to reason things out. This has led to many disasters in this life.

The Voice of the Mind

1. The mind is a great asset for every Christian and every minister.

I believe that the mind is one of the most wonderful gifts that God has given to every man. The mind is one of the most complex computers in the world today. It is a gift that you are expected to use. Even when you are born-again, you are expected to use your mind. When you are a spiritual leader, you are expected to use your mind!

When you want to decide whether to marry someone or not, you must first use your mind. You must ask yourself, "What is the background of this person? How old is he or she? What is the educational background of the person? What is the family background of the person? What language does he or she speak?"

The Difference between Men and Animals

When I have to take decisions in the ministry, I do not just pray about them. I think about them! I analyse things! God gave me a mind and I intend to use it on a daily basis. What is the difference between a human being and an animal? The human being has a more developed brain. This gives him a mind with a great thinking capability. It is the use of the mind, which has made human beings rule and dominate all animals.

We human beings have control over animals that are wild and dangerous. We control poisonous and deadly reptiles by the use of a superior mind. We capture animals like elephants and whales that are a hundred times the size of a man. We keep them in cages and observe them at our pleasure. What gives us this power? It is the use of a superior mind.

The Difference between Men and Men

Even amongst human beings, those that have encouraged the use of the mind have ended up ruling those that have not used their minds much. The educated (developed minds) are ruling the uneducated. Go into almost every institution and you will find that the educated are higher placed than the uneducated. They have higher salaries and are better looked after.

In a very sophisticated world, the inventors of cars and airplanes are dominating millions of people who have not used their minds to create such things. The inventors and manufacturers of televisions, videos and telephones have more money than those who just buy and use them. Through the world's complex financial system, many people who are officially free from slavery are still experiencing a sophisticated form of financial and mental slavery!

Those who know how to convert cocoa beans into chocolate and other niceties have more "say so" than those who just know how to harvest cocoa on a farm. It takes more use of the mind to develop machines and complicated equipment that are used to convert raw materials into final products.

Simply speaking, the world is divided into two: those who have used their God-given gift of a super mind and those who have not!

2. Do not send your mind on vacation because you have become a spiritual person.

Do a survey of some churches. Those who have emphasized on spiritual and emotional things, to the absolute exclusion of rational thinking, have ended up on the rocks. God does not expect you to exclude your mind because you are a spiritual person. I consider myself to be a very spiritual person. I spend numerous hours a week in prayer. I believe that the Bible is my final authority on all matters of doctrine. This however, has not made me to stop reasoning and rationalizing things. When you stop using your mind, even in the spiritual world, you lower yourself from the rank that God intends for you.

How to Cross a Road

Someone wanted to know the will of God about marriage. I said to him, "Do you know the Kaneshie-Mallam Highway (a very wide and dangerous highway in the city of Accra in my country, Ghana)?"

He said, "Yes, I do."

I asked him, "If you wanted to cross that road what would you do?"

He began to answer but I stopped him.

I said to him, "I know what you would do! You would close your eyes and ask the Lord to speak to you and tell you the exact moment to cross."

He smiled.

I continued, "Wouldn't you do that?"

"I don't think so," he responded.

I went on, "If you were to do something like that you are likely to be killed immediately. The highest form of manifested stupidity is to shut off your mind when you are taking important decisions."

I said to him, "God is not the author of foolishness. He does not expect you to close your eyes and listen to the voice of the Spirit telling you when to cross. He gave you eyes to see and a mind with which to make sound judgments. It is like having money in your pocket that God has given you to solve your problems. Yet, you cry to Him and ask Him for money. Meanwhile, you have some money in your pocket.

What is God saying to you? God is saying that it is time to think again. It is time to be educated. It is time to reason. If you are a pastor, do not take all the decisions on your own. When it comes to finances, think and use the minds of trained accountants. When it comes to legal matters, believe and accept the minds of trained lawyers. When it comes to church growth, read and learn everything you can.

3. A combination of the voice of the Spirit and the voice of the mind will lead to your promotion in life and ministry.

The Holy Spirit is not the author of foolishness and absurdities. Please stop claiming that the Spirit is telling you things when that is not the case! There are many things that I do not pray about; I simply *think* about them. The Bible says that Christ is to us not only power but also wisdom.

> ... *Christ the power of God, and the wisdom of God.*
> **1 Corinthians 1:24**

Jesus Christ in our lives makes us wise and not foolish. If you want to be promoted in this life, get wisdom. Wisdom has to do with the mind. The Bible says that wisdom is the principal thing. Therefore, with all your getting, get wisdom.

> *Exalt her [wisdom], and she shall promote thee: she shall bring thee to honour, when thou dost embrace her.*
> **Proverbs 4:8**

Your promotion and honour are on the way when you start applying yourself to God's wisdom. Never forget that it was wisdom that brought Joseph out of jail and into the king's palace. Wisdom brought Daniel into the rank of prime minister and vice-president in three successive governments. It was wisdom and the use of his mind that made Solomon the richest man on earth. **Wisdom is the intelligent use** of your thinking capabilities. Wisdom is the ability to take right decisions based on the information available to you. Wisdom is the ability not to ignore realities when they are before you.

4. Too much reasoning can turn you into a fool.

There is, however, one danger with the voice of the mind – the danger of reasoning until you become foolish again. Knowledge and thinking without God will make you into a fool.

The expositors of the evolution theory reasoned their way through a maze of obvious scientific realities involving the evolution of created beings. They saw some things and propounded some theories. However, when they got to a point where they had to question themselves about the *origin* of *all* created beings, they began to guess and made fools out of themselves.

It is the mother of all absurdities for someone to say that this intricate, fantastic and perfect creation of God came about through an explosion (The Big Bang Theory). In the medical school, I dissected the body of a dead human being for one and a half years. I discovered for myself how extraordinary and awesome God's creation is.

This is why the Bible says it is only a fool who says that there is no God. No one can tell me that an explosion that occurred in Germany created a Mercedes-Benz car. That is foolishness!

Even though you must develop your mind, God's Word and His Spirit are superior to every reasoning of man. You must allow the wisdom of God to supersede the wisdom of man.

> *Where is the wise? where is the scribe? where is the disputer of this world? hath not God made foolish the wisdom of this world?*
> **1 Corinthians 1:20**

> *Because the foolishness of God is wiser than men; and the weakness of God is stronger than men.*
> **1 Corinthians 1:25**

There are times when God will direct you and it will not look wise in the natural. When I left my noble medical profession for the Ministry, many people thought I had gone mad. My parents were distressed and my relatives were worried. They could not see the sense in what I was doing. They asked, "Why should someone leave such a promising career for an apparently fruitless and uncertain adventure?"

But I knew that God had called me and at such times natural reasoning had to give way to the voice of God.

The problem with this is that many Christians are simply not using their minds at all. They continue claiming that every quixotic adventure they embark on is directed by the supernatural voice of God.

It is time to let the voice of your mind have its proper place.

Chapter 8

The Voice of the Bible

The Bible contains the written Word of God. It is a reliable source of direction for us all. The Word of God is a silent voice. How can a voice be silent? The silent voices are a group of voices that the Holy Spirit uses to guide us. They are silent in the sense that you do not hear a person speaking audibly. They are however, common ways by which the Holy Spirit leads us all. You see, being led by the Spirit of God is not a very simple thing. Today, human beings communicate by speech, by touch, by facial expressions, by letters, faxes, telephones, television, e-mail and so on. There are also many methods by which God communicates with His children. One of these is the written Word of God.

The Word of God

The Word of God is given to us for direction in our lives. Everything we do must be done according to the Word of

God. In a very general way, the Word of God is the perfect guidebook for our lives. The Bible is a unique book that contains instruction on every possible issue that may arise. There are many people who think that the Bible is not a practical and relevant book for today.

One lady told me that she believed she could practise fornication because the Bible was out of fashion. Three years later, when her boyfriend of many years ditched her, she realized that the Bible was not so archaic after all.

> *All scripture is given by inspiration of God, and is profitable for doctrine, for reproof, for correction, for instruction in righteousness: That the man of God may be perfect, throughly furnished unto all good works.*
>
> **2 Timothy 3:16, 17**

The Scripture is profitable, useful, relevant and practical for every Christian today! There are many Christians who do not want you to open the Bible; they just want a prophecy or a word of knowledge.

The Word Is a Light

> *… I have ordained a lamp for mine anointed.*
>
> **Psalm 132:17**

Use the Word of God as a light for your path. There is so much darkness in the world. We often do not know what to do, but God has provided a light for Christians. What is this light that God has provided for Christians?

> *Thy word is a lamp unto my feet, and a light unto my path.*
>
> **Psalm 119:105**

God's Word is a lamp and a light for us. It is only when you put on the light that you know where to go. It is only when you put on the light that you can prevent yourself from stumbling over furniture. Jesus Christ called Himself the light of this world.

> *... I am the light of the world: he that followeth me shall not walk in darkness, but shall have the light of life.*
>
> **John 8:12**

You need light in this life! Jesus (the Word) is the light for your life. People who have tried to live their lives without Christ and the Word have discovered that it is painful to stumble around in the darkness.

A young man approached me and informed me that he was having terrible problems in his marriage. He wanted me to help him. He wanted to know the way out of his marital difficulties. As I talked with him, I realized that what he needed was the Word. He said to me, "Are you going to pray for me to have my deliverance?"

I asked, "Why do you need deliverance?"

He answered, "Oh, I was told that my wife has a marine spirit."

I asked him, "What is a marine spirit?"

He said, "Oh, it's something they say I have to be delivered from. So I want you to deliver me." I thought to myself, "This man wants a quick fix. He does not want the Word. He does not know that nothing sets you free like the Word of God does."

> *And ye shall know the truth, and the truth shall make you free.*
>
> **John 8:32**

I asked him, "Are you a born-again Christian?"

"Yes, I am."

"Are you faithful to your wife?" I asked.

He smiled, "Um… not really."

"Actually", he continued, "I have not been faithful to her at all!"

I advised this man to have a pastor and belong to a church. I told him, "Your marine spirit is the least of your problems. What you need is the Word of God to guide you in this life. **You need the light of life; otherwise, you will continue to grope in darkness.**"

There are people who wonder how I know the things I do. I remember arriving in Johannesburg one day for a convention. I was met by a South African delegation. When they saw me, one of them asked, "Are you the Bishop?"

I said, "Yes, I am."

"Really! We were expecting someone much older! We have listened to your tapes and read your books. Somehow, we thought you were a much older person." When you walk in the Word, people will think you are much older than your real age.

The Word Is Wisdom

> *Thou through thy commandments hast made me wiser than mine enemies… I have more understanding than all my teachers: for thy testimonies are my meditation.*
>
> **Psalm 119:98, 99**

The Word of God will make you wise in this life. Advice and direction for business are found in the Word of God. There is more instruction for a businessperson in the Word of God than in any lecture on business management. There is more relevant and practical knowledge on philosophy, political science, literature and history in the Bible than in any other book I know.

The Word Is Instruction

I sometimes smile when people say, "God has called me to do such-and-such for Him." If you do not obey the simple instructions in the Word, do you think God is going to give you more? He that is faithful in little is faithful in much. If you do not obey the Word of God which says to pay your tithes, do you think God is going to speak to you about a miracle healing ministry?

> *He hath shewed thee, O man, what is good; and what doth the LORD require of thee...*
>
> **Micah 6:8**

God will minister His Word to you through pastors and shepherds. That is why it is important to have a good church and a pastor who teaches the Word of God. Whenever your pastor is preaching, be open to receive direction for your life.

The Word Brings Understanding

In the last days, God is giving pastors who will feed us with knowledge and understanding. Receive the knowledge and understanding that God is giving you.

> *And I will give you pastors according to mine heart, which shall feed you with knowledge and understanding.*
>
> **Jeremiah 3:15**

God will also use men of God to give you instructions for your life. These instructions help you to become a better person. There are times your pastor will give a commandment to fast and pray. It is important to follow these instructions. The Bible teaches that we should obey those that have spiritual authority over us.

> *Obey them that have the rule over you, and submit yourselves: for they watch for your souls...*
>
> **Hebrews 13:17**

Listen to the voice of your shepherd. God has delegated the destiny of the sheep to the shepherd. God will bless your life and lead you through the voice of your shepherd. Jesus is the overall shepherd and He told Peter to look after the sheep. That means that He was delegating the care of His sheep to under-shepherds.

> *... Simon, son of Jonas, lovest thou me?... Jesus saith unto him, Feed my sheep.*
>
> **John 21:17**

The Voice of the Shepherd

Since the shepherd speaks the Word of God, the voice of the shepherd contains the light, the understanding and the wisdom that you need.

If you are a sheep, God will lead you through your shepherd. Once you become sheep-like you can expect to receive direction from your shepherd. "My sheep know my voice and they follow me." Your shepherd will explain the Bible to you. Through the words of the shepherd, the Bible will come alive in your life.

One of the surest ways God can direct you is through the person who acts as your shepherd. This shepherd is your pastor. Be very careful with the words of your pastor. They are the anointed words of a shepherd to the sheep. They contain all the guidance that the sheep needs.

Chapter 9

Five Keys to Victory over the Voice of Your Flesh

Remember These Keys

1. The voice of your flesh is your human desire.

2. The voice of your flesh is your physical feelings.

3. The voice of the flesh says, "Do what feels nice and easy."

4. Do not obey the voice of the flesh if you want to be blessed.

5. You can silence the voice of the flesh by doing what is hard and difficult.

The voice of your flesh is the expression of your desires and feelings. Whenever you have certain feelings and desires, the flesh is speaking. The flesh is a very dangerous thing to follow. If you follow your desires for food, rest and sex, you will end up as a spiritual disaster.

> *For to be carnally minded is death; but to be spiritually minded is life and peace.*
>
> **Romans 8:6**

A spiritual person is someone who grows to the point where he is able to realize when his flesh is speaking or influencing him. Jesus said, "The spirit is willing but the flesh is weak" (Matthew 26:41). The flesh always wants to do the wrong thing. It constantly influences you along the course of least resistance.

I have realized that if I do the things that are hard and difficult, I get to be promoted. Whereas, if I do the things which are nice and easy, I do not progress. The flesh wants you to sleep. It is your flesh that will say to you, "Do not go to that all-night prayer meeting."

Many young men should know that it is actually the desire of the flesh that motivates them towards marriage and relationships. Often, young men are not led by the Spirit into marriage but by their flesh!

A Special Ministry

Some years ago, as a student in Achimota School (a secondary school in Ghana), I noticed a young man who called himself a minister. He would come to the school to visit us and to minister the Word.

After a while, I observed that this man hardly ever visited the brothers in the boarding school. He could always be found chatting with the ladies and "ministering" to them. One day I asked him, "How come you hardly come to see the brothers anymore?"

I added, "You spend all your time at the girls' dormitory."

"Oh," he answered, "I have a special call from God. My ministry is to the sisters."

In other words, God had called him to spend all his time with the ladies.

At that time, I accepted it as a valid ministry. However, if you study the Bible, you will not find such a ministry. The Bible says that the older women should teach the younger women (Titus 2:4).

This fellow was probably just following the natural dictates of his flesh. As a man, he tended to flow more with the sisters. This is a natural phenomenon. It happens all the time. But instead of acknowledging the reality of his flesh and what was natural, he claimed that the Holy Spirit had given him a *special ministry* to girls.

The "Spirit" Speaks?

A young man was sent out by the General Superintendent of his denomination to pioneer a church in the metropolis. This young man was poorly educated and had no steady job. He was however operating as a lay pastor (an unpaid/voluntary minister). He began the church by witnessing and following-up the converts. To his surprise, the church began to grow. The church's growth was aided by the good name of that ministry. He also flowed in the general anointing that was over that denomination.

The church that had begun in the young man's sitting room soon grew until there were over one hundred members in the church. The money began to roll in and for the first time, the church's bank account had over one million cedis (five hundred dollars at the 1999 exchange rate). After a while, the man who said that the church should meet in his house free of charge came up with an outrageous sum, as rent owed him. This pastor had obviously seen the financial capacity and capability of the church. The church had more money than he thought it would ever have.

The denomination's administrators however, refused to pay that huge sum of money. They offered to pay a smaller sum of money. The rent issue then died a natural death. However, a couple of months later the pastor suddenly requested an audience with the General Superintendent of the church.

"What can we do for you?" the Superintendent asked.

"The Lord has spoken to me. He has asked me to resign from this ministry and to begin my own church," the pastor revealed.

The surprised Superintendent queried, "What do you mean?"

"It's nothing personal. God has called me. He said I should start my own ministry."

"I see," said the Superintendent, "Are you sure there is no other reason?"

"No! The Spirit of God has spoken and I have to obey!"

The administrators of the church questioned this pastor, "Is it not because you want control over the church's money? Are you not taking this decision for financial reasons?"

The pastor was not pleased, "Are you doubting my call? Do you doubt that God has spoken to me?"

This pastor eventually took over the church, changed its name and stole the entire congregation. The denomination decided to start another church nearby for those of its members who wanted to remain loyal to the denomination.

A week after this pastor had stolen the congregation, it came to light that he had been siphoning money from the church offerings. Instead of following the clearly laid down rules of his denomination (to bank all monies immediately), he would take some money out and use it. In other words, he was making wrong declarations of the church's offerings.

This is an example of someone who claimed that he had heard the voice of God. Although no one can really judge, it is quite obvious that there were many financial considerations in this young pastor's decision to break away from his denomination.

The voice of the flesh crying out for more money was being heard loud and clear. Learn to distinguish the voice of the flesh from other voices.

> *There are, it may be, so many kinds of voices in the world, and none of them is without signification.*
>
> **1 Corinthians 14:10**

Chapter 10

Three Things You Should Know about the Voice of the Holy Spirit

The voice of the Holy Spirit is the most important voice that we need to hear in these times. Jesus said that He would send us the Holy Spirit to guide us. The Holy Spirit speaks the mind of God.

> *... for he shall not speak of himself; but whatsoever he shall hear, that shall he speak: and he will shew you things to come.*
>
> **John 16:13**

1. The voice of the Holy Spirit transmits God's current plan for you.

One of the cardinal duties of the Holy Spirit is to transmit God's mind to you. He will not speak of Himself. Whatever He hears God say, He will relay it to you. From today, there is no need to consult the astrologers or the stars. The Holy Spirit will show you things to come.

God will tell you what to expect. If He does not tell you anything, then there is nothing unusual to expect. The Holy Spirit is on duty twenty-four hours a day; He speaks all the time. It is our duty therefore to learn about His voice and how to distinguish it from other voices.

2. The Holy Spirit may choose to speak to your spirit, soul or body.

The Holy Spirit has a voice. However, the Bible teaches that He speaks directly to your spirit, soul or body. When the Holy Spirit speaks to your mind, it will sound a little different from when He speaks to your physical body.

I have experienced the voice of the Holy Spirit speaking to me in all three ways. He speaks to us in all three ways and it is important for us to receive from the Holy Spirit in whichever way He chooses to speak to us. When the Holy Spirit speaks to your spirit, you do not hear an audible voice. This is what people call "the inner witness".

3. The voice of the Holy Spirit to your spirit is called the "Inner Witness".

The Bible also tells us that the Holy Spirit is in our hearts (spirit) crying "Abba Father", which is the cry of a child to his real father. By the voice of the Holy Spirit in your heart, you know that you are a real child of God.

> *And because ye are sons, God hath sent forth THE SPIRIT of his Son into your hearts, CRYING, Abba, Father.*
>
> **Galatians 4:6**

This verse says that the Holy Spirit is crying or shouting in your heart. But have you ever heard an audible voice saying "Abba Father"? Have you ever had an audible voice flashing through your mind saying "Abba Father"? The answer is no! What is the effect of the Holy Spirit crying "Abba Father" in our heart? It creates a silent assurance of your salvation. You know that you are a Christian and you know that you are going to Heaven.

The voice of the Holy Spirit to your spirit creates what I call a *quiet* assurance. It creates a *relaxed knowing* about something. Apostle Paul described this as *perceiving* or a *knowing*. You may ask, "Pastor, how do you know these things?" I know it from the Bible. Let us read it together.

> *Now when much time was spent, and when sailing was now dangerous, because the fast was now already past, Paul admonished them, And said unto them, Sirs, I PERCEIVE that this voyage will be with hurt and much damage, not only of the lading and ship, but also of our lives. Nevertheless the centurion believed the master and the owner of the ship, more than those things which were spoken by Paul.*
>
> **Acts 27:9-11**

Apostle Paul declared to the Centurion and other experienced sailors that he perceived that there were going to be serious problems during the journey. Paul did not say that he had heard the Spirit of God telling him not to travel. He just had a *knowing* and a *perception*. How did he know this? How did he perceive this? Was it a natural perception or a spiritual perception? It was definitely not a natural perception because in the natural there was no sign of danger. The wind was blowing very softly, which was a good sign.

> *And when the south wind blew softly, supposing that they had obtained their purpose, loosing thence, they sailed close by Crete.*
>
> **Acts 27:13**

As you can see, the south wind was blowing softly. There was no indication of trouble. Paul had what many Christians have when the Holy Spirit speaks to their spirit – *a perception and a knowing.* As if to distinguish between the different ways in which the Holy Spirit speaks, the Lord spoke to Paul in a different way on this same journey.

The bad things he had perceived had happened and the people on the ship had given up hope of surviving. However, God spoke to Paul in an unusual or spectacular way.

> *But after long abstinence Paul stood forth in the midst of them, and said, Sirs, ye should have hearkened unto me, and not have loosed from Crete, and to have gained this harm and loss. And now I exhort you to be of good cheer: for there shall be no loss of any man's life among you, but of the ship. For THERE STOOD BY ME THIS NIGHT THE ANGEL OF GOD, whose I am, and whom I serve, Saying, Fear not, Paul; thou must be brought before Caesar: and, lo, God hath*

> *given thee all them that sail with thee. Wherefore, sirs, be of good cheer: for I believe God, that it shall be even as it was told me.*
>
> **Acts 27:21-25**

You can see from this passage that the Holy Spirit spoke in two different ways on two different occasions. The first time was by the inner witness and the second time was by an angel.

Another Scripture which says the same thing is Romans 8:16.

> *The Spirit itself beareth witness with our spirit, that we are the children of God:*
>
> **Romans 8:16**

When the Holy Spirit speaks to your spirit, you do not have thoughts flashing through your mind. The Spirit bearing witness is the same as the Spirit speaking or witnessing to your heart that you are a child of God. This is the commonest way that you will detect the voice of the Spirit. When you want to take a decision, watch out for that quiet assurance in your heart! If you want to marry somebody, watch out for that relaxed *knowing* that "this is it!" If you need to change your job or enter a partnership, check up on whether you have that quiet assurance of peace in your heart.

Chapter 11

Seven Characteristics of the Inner Witness

The Spirit itself BEARETH WITNESS WITH OUR SPIRIT, that we are the children of God:

Romans 8:16

And because ye are sons, God hath sent forth THE SPIRIT of his Son into your hearts, CRYING, Abba, Father.

Galatians 4:6

The question is, "How can I distinguish the voice of this inner witness? Are there any features that I must look out for? What differentiates the inner witness from an ordinary thought?" I want to give you seven characteristics that you must look out for.

1. The inner witness is different from reasoning thoughts.

It is not mental knowledge or logical reasoning. If what you are having is just an ingenious idea, then it's probably not the inner witness.

2. The inner witness is not a physical feeling.

Because the inner witness is the voice of the Holy Spirit to your spirit, you will not have a physical feeling per se. If someone claims that he has a physical feeling in his big toe or his liver that is probably not the inner witness!

3. The inner witness is best identified by eliminating other voices.

A great secret to identifying the inner witness is to eliminate other voices. Ensure that it is not your flesh that wants to do something. Make sure that it is not just a reasonable proposition. There may be some good reason and some good feelings when the Spirit is leading you, but make sure it is not just that!

4. The inner witness is an impression of peace.

The inner witness is an awareness of peace. It is the peace of God that is beyond (passes) understanding, reasoning, logic and physical things. As you develop spiritually you will become aware of the peace of God as a method of direction. You will say, "I don't have peace about this!" At other times you will say, "Even though it sounds odd, I have peace about this issue. I know it shall be well with me."

5. The inner witness is a strong conviction.

The inner witness makes you certain about what the Lord is saying. You begin to have a quiet assurance and confidence about the will of God.

Once again, this is not easily explained. Do you think people who give up their lives for the gospel can explain what they are doing? You cannot easily explain the faith you have! You cannot always explain the convictions you have!

6. The inner witness is repetitive.

The inner witness is the repeated voice of the Holy Spirit speaking to your heart.

> *… the Spirit… crying…*
>
> **Galatians 4:6**

As the Spirit cries continually, it creates an impression in you. You begin to have a conviction about certain things. You begin to know that you know. One characteristic that I have noticed is that the voice of the Spirit is repeated over and over. This happens over several weeks, months and even years.

7. The inner witness is an inexplicable knowing.

After you have heard the voice of the Spirit several times, you begin to know what to do. It creates in you a *knowing*. Sometimes people ask me, "How did you know what to do?" Sometimes all I can say is, "I just knew."

Chapter 12

How to Use "Peace the Umpire" for Daily Guidance

Paul described the phenomenon of the inner witness in a peculiar way. He called the peace of God "an umpire". In other words, we have a special referee in our lives who guides us.

> *And let the PEACE of God RULE in your hearts...*
> **Colossians 3:15**

The peace of God in our hearts is supposed to rule or guide us. The peace of God in our hearts is generated by the voice of the Holy Spirit speaking to our hearts. When you don't have that peace, please be careful of danger. The Greek word translated "rule" is the word *brabeuo*. It means "to be an umpire", "to arbitrate", "to direct" and "to govern".

God is using peace to direct and govern you. I say to you, "If you don't have peace, don't go! If you don't have peace about him, don't marry him!" Peace is the umpire you have!

When the umpire blows the whistle, you are supposed to stop.

It is the umpire who tells you to "play on". He signals to you when something is wrong. If you learn to follow this peace in your heart, you will experience success in all decisions that you take.

A friend of mine left church one evening and stopped a taxi on a motorway. He told me later of a terrible experience he had. He said, "I remember that as I was getting into the car I felt very uneasy. I had no peace." You see, peace the umpire was blowing the whistle and telling him, "No! Don't go!"

He narrated, "There was one person in addition to the driver. I was sitting on the back seat."

In the middle of the journey the driver began to drive very slowly. He turned off his lights and began to sing a hymn, *Lead kindly light* (a song that is often sung at funerals). The driver revealed himself to be a wizard who was operating from a town near the capital, Accra. As they drove along, the driver and the man in front said to my friend, "We are taking you somewhere."

He was terrified. They turned off the motorway onto a dusty road and drove into a cemetery. When they arrived at the cemetery they told him, "Get out of the car. You are going to die."

My friend said to me, "I knew that this was my last hour. They said that they were going to sacrifice me and use parts of my body for rituals."

He continued, "Just before they were about to sacrifice me, I prayed, knowing that these were my last minutes on earth."

The driver of the car then said, "If you will join our witchcraft group, I will not kill you."

My friend told me, "I agreed to join for the sake of my life."

Thinking that they had got a convert they went back to the car and drove to the next town. My friend told me, "They dropped me off at the nearest junction in the town centre. When I got out of the car I told the man, "If you think I would ever join such an evil group, you must be out of your mind. The power of Jesus is greater than any power."

And with that he ran off into the nearby crowd. The driver could not pursue him because there were too many people around.

God had saved my friend from certain death at the hands of ritual murderers. But God had tried to direct him through the umpire called peace. The uneasiness my friend had felt when he was getting into the car was a warning from God not to proceed.

In the ministry, you need to have peace about many things that you engage in. Sometimes there is no reason for peace. Sometimes you don't know why you are at peace. The Bible calls it "the peace that passes all understanding".

Chapter 13

How to Tell the Difference When the Spirit Speaks in Different Ways

The Voice of the Holy Spirit to Your Soul (Mind)

The Holy Spirit also speaks to our minds and directs us. What is it like when the Holy Spirit speaks to your mind? Anything that enters your mind is a thought. The Holy Spirit speaks to your mind by bringing thoughts to it.

> But the Comforter, which is the Holy Ghost, whom the Father will send in my name, he shall teach you all things, and bring all things to your remembrance [mind], whatsoever I have said unto you.
>
> **John 14:26**

This verse states clearly that the Holy Spirit will bring things to your mind. You must learn to distinguish between thoughts that come from your natural thought processes and thoughts that come from the Holy Spirit. There are also thoughts and suggestions that come from Satan.

Someone asked, "How do you know the voice of the Holy Spirit?" That is like asking, "How do I know the voice of my wife? Or for that matter anyone else?" By experience! The more I hear certain voices, the more easily I can identify them. Certain people call me on the telephone and do not need to introduce themselves. I know who they are when they begin to speak.

When you become conversant with the voice of the Holy Spirit to your spirit, soul or body, you will know when He speaks. I have many thoughts passing through my mind all the time. Just like everyone else, I have to filter these and decide which ones are natural and which ones are supernatural.

How I Heard That Voice in My Mind

Some years ago, I was dealing with a rebellious individual in my church. I felt strongly that this pastor was a rebel and that he was a liar. However, he had denied it on so many occasions that I doubted within myself whether this was the case. One day, while on a trip to Europe, the Holy Spirit spoke to my mind. I was lying down in bed when the Spirit of God spoke clearly into my mind. He said, "So-and-so is a liar and I will show you five different lies he has told you at different times."

Suddenly and in rapid succession, the Holy Spirit gave me five clear instances when this pastor had lied to me. They came so fast that I struggled to remember them afterwards. Then the Holy Spirit said, "Because of these, know that he is lying to you about this current problem." That was the turning point in my relationship with that particular minister. I suddenly knew that I was dealing with a prevaricator who by evasive and misleading answers had been able to live a lie.

God showed me that day that I had to deal with this rebellious and contumacious young man. And I did just that!

If you are a pastor, you will need the Spirit of God to lead you especially in relation to those who work with you. The spirit of Judas is the spirit of the perfect pretender. Sometimes you will never know of the deadly poison around you unless God reveals it to you supernaturally. I have found that the Spirit of God does these unusual things when there is no way for me to know certain things naturally! It is not the principal way that God speaks to you, but it is certainly an important method.

God speaks to your mind when He has to. The Bible makes it clear.

> ... [He will] bring all things to your remembrance [mind], whatsoever I have said unto you.
>
> **John 14:26**

Many times when men of God say that God has spoken to them, they mean that certain thoughts came to their mind which they believe are from the Holy Spirit.

From today, have faith in the voice of the Holy Spirit speaking to your mind.

The Spirit of God says things to your mind (remembrance). When He speaks to your mind, you have distinctive, special and unique thoughts. It comes in a way that is unusual. It is learnt through experience and operated by faith.

The Voice of the Holy Spirit to Your Body

And as he journeyed, he came near Damascus: and suddenly there shined round about him a light from heaven: And he fell to the earth, and heard a voice saying unto him, Saul, Saul, why persecutest thou me? And he said, Who art thou, Lord? And the Lord said, I am Jesus whom thou persecutest: it is hard for thee to kick against the pricks.

Acts 9:3-5

You must also learn the voice of the Holy Spirit speaking to your physical being. *In this case, you will hear an audible voice speaking to you.* The Bible is full of such examples; however, do not make the mistake of thinking that it was an everyday occurrence with the Apostles.

Paul probably heard the voice of the Holy Spirit speaking to him in this way only once or twice in his lifetime. There is no need to seek these spectacular experiences. The devil knows when you have an appetite for sensational things. He is an expert at filling you with deception when he knows that you are vulnerable.

I have walked with the Lord for over twenty years. Once in my life, I believe I heard the audible voice of the Holy Spirit speaking to me. But that is not the principal way by which the Holy Spirit leads me.

I believe I am called to the ministry. The proof of my call is in the fact that you are reading this book now! However, the Holy Spirit did not speak to me audibly to call me into the ministry. I have the quiet assurance of the voice of the Holy Spirit speaking to my heart. I know that I must be in the ministry. I know that I must not do anything else with my life. I must preach until I die. Like Paul said, "Woe is me if I preach not the Gospel." God does not need to give you a dramatic experience before you start obeying Him.

At different stages of my ministry, the Spirit has spoken to me in different ways. As far back as 1980, in Achimota Secondary School, I can remember the Spirit of God speaking to my spirit and giving me that inner knowing and peace about doing His work. Because of this, I have the conviction to serve God in the ministry as a pastor. It is this relaxed assurance that has put me in the ministry.

In 1988, in a remote village hospital of Ghana, the Spirit of God spoke to me audibly and showed me the direction to take in the ministry. In June 1996, in a small French village, the Spirit spoke to my mind and told me to start operating in certain areas of the ministry.

At each stage of my life the Holy Spirit has spoken to me in whatever way He found appropriate. He will also speak to you and you will get to know His voice as you walk with Him.

Chapter 14

Four Reasons for Spectacular Guidance

We now come to more spectacular forms of guidance by the Holy Spirit. These include things like dreams, visions, trances, the appearance of angels and even the appearance of Jesus. We must ask ourselves why God chooses different methods each time. God is sovereign; He can decide to do whatever He wants.

I am not attempting to give a formula for how God speaks. I am just showing some patterns I have found in the Word of God. I would like to share with you four reasons why God may choose to speak to you in a spectacular way.

Four Reasons

1. God may speak in a spectacular way because it involves something very important for your life and ministry.

2. God may speak in a spectacular way because all other methods to reach you have not worked.

3. God may speak in a spectacular way because He sometimes shows mercy to stubborn people.

4. God may speak in a spectacular way because it involves something very important for His church.

Spectacular Guidance for Salvation

The Apostle Paul is an example of someone who experienced spectacular guidance. By the way, the fact that the guidance may not be spectacular does not mean it's not supernatural. Paul's salvation was not a typical case of conversion. I believe there are three reasons why God spoke to Paul in a spectacular way.

a. Paul was destroying the church.

Who was before... injurious...

1 Timothy 1:13

b. God wanted to show mercy to a stubborn person.

Who was before a blasphemer...

1 Timothy 1:13

c. God wanted to save Paul's life because no one can destroy the church and get away with it.

> ... it is hard for thee to kick against the pricks.
>
> **Acts 9:5**

Spectacular Guidance for Joining the Right Church (Company)

Shortly after Paul's dramatic conversion, the Lord used another spectacular method to lead Paul into the right church so that he could have the right training for the ministry. Paul was a proud lawyer who might have thought that a few humble Jews could not teach him much.

> ... for one called Saul, of Tarsus: for, behold, he prayeth, And hath seen in a vision a man named Ananias coming in, and putting his hand on him, that he might receive his sight.
>
> **Acts 9:11, 12**

The visions surrounding Paul's direction to join the main church were so dramatic that Paul couldn't help but listen to the counsel of older and more experienced Christians. I believe that God did this because it involved the future ministry to the entire "Gentile" world.

Spectacular Guidance for Where to Start a Church

One day Paul made plans to travel to Bithynia. He wanted to start a ministry there, but the Spirit of God had other plans. That night the Spirit of God spoke to Paul in a vision. He saw a man standing in Macedonia and saying, "Come over into Macedonia, and help us." Once again, this was very important for the building of the church.

Spectacular Guidance for Survival

Further on in Paul's ministry a situation arose which threatened his very life. He was about to die in a shipwreck (plane crash). An angel suddenly appeared and told him what to do.

> *But after long abstinence Paul stood forth in the midst of them, and said, Sirs, ye should have hearkened unto me, and not have loosed from Crete, and to have gained this harm and loss. And now I exhort you to be of good cheer: for there shall be no loss of any man's life among you, but of the ship. For there stood by me this night the angel of God, whose I am, and whom I serve, Saying, Fear not, Paul; thou must be brought before Caesar: and, lo, God hath given thee all them that sail with thee. Wherefore, sirs, be of good cheer: for I believe God, that it shall be even as it was told me.*
> **Acts 27:21-25**

Because of the angelic visitation, Paul directed everyone to eat some food. This saved their lives and enabled them to survive until they ran aground.

As you can see, one or more of the four reasons given at the beginning of this chapter is always present when God speaks in a spectacular way.

Spectacular Guidance to Help You Endure a Difficult Season

Paul was going to go through a very difficult period as a prisoner. He was about to be arrested and kept in prison cells until he died. This was an important part of Paul's ministry because it was there that he wrote many of his letters. It is by these letters that Paul's ministry has lived on for two thousand years.

> *And as we tarried there many days, there came down from Judaea a certain prophet, named Agabus. And when he was come unto us, he took Paul's girdle, and bound his own hands and feet, and said, Thus saith the Holy Ghost, So shall the Jews at Jerusalem bind the man that owneth this girdle, and shall deliver him into the hands of the Gentiles.*
>
> **Acts 21:10, 11**

Chapter 15

How to Identify a Door

… Behold, I have set before thee an open door…
Revelation 3:8

1. An open door is a God-given opportunity in the midst of impossibilities.

2. An open door is a chance to escape or to achieve something for the Lord.

3. An open door is an opening in the midst of impassable circumstances.

4. An open door is a time-related breakthrough that gives you a needed option.

Three Ways to Recognize a Door

1. **The first way to recognize a door is to recognize an opportunity that comes in the midst of other unworkable options.**

In the natural, a door is flanked on the left and right by impenetrable walls. This reveals impossible or impenetrable circumstances all around except in the position where the door is.

> *... I will tarry at Ephesus... For A GREAT DOOR and effectual is opened...*
>
> **1 Corinthians 16:8, 9**

Paul decided to remain at Ephesus because of the opportunities to minister over there. All around him were hostile cities that were not open to the gospel. **When you are *flanked* by impossibilities and one niche opens up, it is often God opening a door for you.**

2. **The second way to recognize a door is to discern that it is an opportunity that will not always be there.**

In the natural, a door does not have a fixed position. It is either open or closed. Any opportunity that appears for a season and disappears again must be considered as a door.

> *... I will tarry at Ephesus... For A GREAT DOOR and effectual is OPENED...*
>
> **1 Corinthians 16:8, 9**

Even though there was an opportunity for ministry at Ephesus, that opportunity would not be there forever. Today, there is very little opportunity for ministry in Ephesus. The door is shut in many parts of Europe. However, the door is now open in many parts of Africa and the developing world. These doors will not remain open forever. Instability and war may close them one day. It is our duty to go through the doors when they swing open. When the "Iron Curtain" came down, there was a sudden open door for the Gospel in Eastern Europe. This door is gradually closing again.

3. The third way to recognize a door is to realize that God engineered the opportunity and that it had nothing to do with your efforts.

In the natural, you do not often construct the doors you meet. Everyone just passes through the doors that are open. An open door is not of your own making, it is just something that you benefit from.

> *And when they were come, and had gathered the church together, they rehearsed all that God had done with them, and how HE HAD OPENED THE DOOR of faith unto the Gentiles.*
>
> **Acts 14:27**

When Paul and Barnabas gave the report of their first missionary journey, everyone was overjoyed at what the Lord had done. They came to one conclusion: God had opened a door to the Gentiles! They knew that only God could do it! That is how to recognize a door. Recognize that it is only God who could have made that opportunity possible.

The Door of Service

There are some important doors that every Christian must recognize and pass through. God often uses doors to direct His children.

> *But I will tarry at Ephesus until Pentecost. For a great door and effectual is opened unto me, and there are many adversaries.*
>
> **1 Corinthians 16:8, 9**

The door of service is the opportunity to be effective for the Lord. The door of service is the opportunity to serve the Lord. We cannot effectively win souls for Jesus all the time. A time comes when it is not possible anymore. Sometimes marriage, pregnancy and childbearing close the door of service. If you grasp the opportunity whilst it is there, you will experience many blessings. When you follow the door of service, you gain two important qualifications. These are:

a. You graduate from being a novice.

God does not put inexperienced people into the ministry. You need experience to be effective as a minister. *What have* you been through? What have you survived? What have you suffered?

> Not a novice, lest being lifted up with pride he fall into the condemnation of the devil.
>
> **1 Timothy 3:6**

b. You prove yourself so that you can be put into an office.

There are four levels in the line of God's service.

- Level one – doing the work. "... do the work of an evangelist..." (2 Timothy 4:5).

- Level two – having a gift. "Having then gifts differing..." (Romans 12:6)

- Level three – having a ministry. "... make full proof of thy ministry" (2 Timothy 4:5).

- Level four – occupying an office. "... I magnify mine office" (Romans 11:13).

Take the evangelistic line of ministry. You could do the work of an evangelist, but that does not mean that you are in the *office* of an evangelist. Like Timothy, you may be temporarily getting involved in the *work* of evangelism. At the next level, you could have a *gift* of evangelism. That does not mean that you are in the ministry of an evangelist, but with an additional step, you could progress into the *ministry* of an evangelist. At this point, it has become your permanent line of service.

At the highest level, you could actually be in the *office* of an evangelist. When you occupy an office, you are at the highest level in that line of ministry. When you are at the office level, you need to employ people to assist you. When there are several people helping and serving under you in your line of ministry, it is often a sign that you are occupying a spiritual *office*.

> *And let these also first be proved; then let them use the office of a deacon, being found blameless.*
>
> **1 Timothy 3:10**

The door of service will show that you are faithful in little things. Then you can be trusted with greater things.

> *He that is faithful in that which is least is faithful also in much...*
>
> **Luke 16:10**

As you follow the doors of service, you will often find yourself doing menial jobs in the ministry. You may be in the background. You may not be seen or praised for what you do, but do not be worried, your reward is guaranteed. The reward for those who went and those who stayed behind is the same. This is a law that was established by King David.

> *... but as his part is that GOETH down to the battle, so shall his part be that TARRIETH by the stuff: THEY SHALL PART ALIKE.*
>
> **1 Samuel 30:24**

How to Recognize a Door of Utterance

Withal praying also for us, that God would open unto us a door of utterance, to speak the mystery of Christ…

Colossians 4:3

The Door of Utterance

A door of utterance is an opportunity to preach or teach. Every opportunity to share the Word must be seized. It is a God-given chance to minister. Any time you share the Word you become more mature. Did you know that the preacher is the one who is most affected by the sermon?

The more you preach, the better you become at ministry. A door of utterance is a door of excellence for you.

The Door of Faith

And when they were come, and had gathered the church together, they rehearsed all that God had done with them, and how he had opened the door of faith unto the Gentiles.

Acts 14:27

A door of faith is the opportunity for salvation for someone. As you relate with people you must discern whether a door of faith is being opened. In Europe for instance, the door of faith (salvation) is shut. This does not mean that people cannot be saved in Europe. But the opportunity for salvation is much greater in some other places.

Sometimes someone goes through a personal crisis and becomes more open to the message of Christ. A door of faith is being opened unto that person. Seize the opportunity and minister the gospel to him.

Chapter 16

What Every Christian Should Know about Dreams

All of us have had dreams from the time that we were very young. Dreams are so common that many Christians have grown up not respecting dreams as a valid method by which God leads us. We seem to think that after all, we had all kinds of dreams as children and also as unbelievers, and we wonder how God can lead us through dreams.

Dreams from the Holy Spirit

Surprisingly, God's Word teaches us that the coming of the Holy Spirit will bring dreams into our lives.

> *And it shall come to pass in the last days, saith God, I will pour out of my Spirit upon all flesh: and your sons and your daughters shall prophesy, and your young*

> *men shall see visions, and your old men shall dream dreams:*
>
> **Acts 2:17**

You can see from this Scripture that dreams come as a direct result of the presence of the Holy Spirit. From today, do not take dreams lightly! This however, does not discount the fact that dreams can come from sources other than the Holy Spirit.

We will examine this also, but what must be established in your heart is the reality that many dreams are the result of the presence of the Holy Spirit. In the book of Job, God reveals that He speaks in dreams when He cannot get our attention. An unusual dream is always something that gets our attention.

> *For God speaketh once, yea twice, yet man perceiveth it not.*
>
> **Job 33:14**

There are times when God may speak to us, but we don't seem to hear. The Bible goes on to say,

> *IN A DREAM, in a vision of the night, when deep sleep falleth upon men, in slumberings upon the bed; THEN HE OPENETH THE EARS OF MEN, and sealeth their instruction,*
>
> **Job 33:15, 16**

Sometimes you wake up in the morning with an unusual dream. It may be that God is trying to get your attention. From today, do not despise dreams. If you consider the birth of Jesus, you will discover how dreams played an important role in the life of Joseph and Mary.

It was a dream that led Joseph to marry Mary, in spite of the fact that she was found to be pregnant before they were married.

> *But while he thought on these things, behold, the angel of the Lord appeared unto him in a dream, saying, Joseph, thou son of David, fear not to take unto thee Mary thy wife: for that which is conceived in her is of the Holy Ghost. And she shall bring forth a son, and thou shalt call his name JESUS: for he shall save his people from their sins.*
>
> **Matthew 1:20, 21**

It was through a dream that Joseph was directed to flee into Egypt for the safety of the baby Jesus. Because Joseph obeyed this dream, Jesus escaped the slaughter of babies that was ordered by Herod.

> *And when they were departed, behold, the angel of the Lord appeareth to Joseph in a dream, saying, Arise, and take the young child and his mother, and flee into Egypt, and be thou there until I bring thee word: for Herod will seek the young child to destroy him.*
>
> **Matthew 2:13**

When Herod died, God spoke yet again by a dream and asked Joseph to return to the land of Israel.

> *But when Herod was dead, behold, an angel of the Lord appeareth in a dream to Joseph in Egypt, Saying, Arise, and take the young child and his mother, and go into the land of Israel: for they are dead which sought the young child's life.*
>
> **Matthew 2:19, 20**

Joseph was directed yet again to move away from Judea into Galilee and into a city called Nazareth. Because of this, Jesus was called a Nazarene.

> *... being warned of God in a dream, he turned aside into the parts of Galilee: And he came and dwelt in a city called Nazareth...*
>
> **Matthew 2:22, 23**

Joseph had *four* dreams in all. By following the direction that he received in each dream, the perfect will of God was done. Prophecies were fulfilled and the Scriptures were confirmed because a man obeyed a dream.

The Apostle Paul was careful to take note of important dreams and visions. He stated that he did not disobey heavenly visions.

> *Whereupon, O king Agrippa, I was NOT DISOBEDIENT UNTO THE HEAVENLY VISION:*
>
> **Acts 26:19**

Paul was someone who respected the voice of God that came to him. It is important for you to accept the fact that God does speak to us through dreams. A "vision in the night" is another biblical description for a dream.

> *And a vision appeared to Paul in the night; There stood a man of Macedonia, and prayed him, saying, Come over into Macedonia, and help us. And after he had seen the vision, immediately we endeavoured to go into Macedonia, assuredly gathering that the Lord had called us for to preach the gospel unto them.*
>
> **Acts 16:9, 10**

From this Scripture, notice how Paul became assured of what to do. One of the ways by which the Holy Spirit leads us is through a dream.

Apostle Peter had an important dream that changed the course of his ministry. Peter was praying on the rooftop while the ladies prepared food downstairs. Whilst praying, he fell into a trance and had a quick dream. In this dream he saw many strange animals and heard a voice saying, "Rise, Peter; kill and eat."

> *On the morrow, as they went on their journey, and drew nigh unto the city, Peter went up upon the housetop to pray about the sixth hour: And he became very hungry, and would have eaten: but while they made ready, he fell into a trance, And saw heaven opened, and a certain vessel descending unto him, as it had been a great sheet knit at the four corners, and let down to the earth: Wherein were all manner of fourfooted beasts of the earth, and wild beasts, and*

> *creeping things, and fowls of the air. And there came a voice to him, Rise, Peter; kill, and eat. But Peter said, Not so, Lord; for I have never eaten any thing that is common or unclean. And the voice spake unto him again the second time, What God hath cleansed, that call not thou common. This was done thrice: and the vessel was received up again into heaven.*
>
> **Acts 10:9-16**

This trance or short dream that Peter had was an important instruction from God to the head of His church. God was telling Peter to go and minister to the Gentiles.

There are times when, just like Peter, you may fall asleep while you are praying. Always take note of the dreams you have at such times. They may be Spirit-inspired messages from the Lord.

Chapter 17

How to Interpret Different Kinds of Dreams

The problem with dreams is that there are four different types of dreams and that can confuse us. Sometimes, because of multiple meaningless dreams, many mature Christians tend to totally ignore the importance of dreams. The four types of dreams are:

i. Dreams from the Holy Spirit

ii. Dreams from your daily activities

iii. Dreams from the flesh

iv. Dreams from the devil.

Dreams from Your Daily Activities

These are dreams that emanate from your everyday activities. The Bible teaches us that a dream comes as a result of our activities or businesses.

> *For a dream cometh through the multitude of business...*
>
> **Ecclesiastes 5:3**

Maybe you were out the entire day with a certain Christian gentleman. A few days later or perhaps that very evening, you have a dream that you were getting married to him. Although this dream could have come from the Holy Spirit, it is more likely that it came as a result of your interaction with him.

Whenever you have a dream, check to see if there is any relationship between your dream and what is going on in your life. It does not have to be something that has happened in your life that very day. It sometimes takes a few weeks before your business activities give rise to a dream.

You must be careful not to say a dream comes from the Holy Spirit when it has come from your own activities. In addition to this, a dream from God must be taken in context with the other ways in which the Holy Spirit speaks.

If the Holy Spirit is speaking to you in a dream, ask yourself whether it lines up with the peace of God in your heart (peace the umpire).

Dreams from the Flesh

One of the common dreams that people experience is having sexual intercourse with another person. Many times those who have such dreams interpret it to mean that they are "spiritually married" to somebody else. However, these dreams are often a night-time continuation of fleshly lusts.

Often the individual involved has experienced several sexual encounters with people. Such dreams sometimes reveal the state of our minds and hearts.

> *Likewise also these filthy dreamers defile the flesh, despise dominion, and speak evil of dignities.*
>
> **Jude 8**

There is something known as a filthy dream and there are people who are filthy dreamers. These people defile the flesh. In other words, they make it dirty. It is time to stop placing the blame on a "marine spirit" or a curse. It is time to face up to the reality that filthy dreams come from a carnal nature that has been allowed to have its way time and time again.

Paul said that he controlled his flesh. Paul had a carnal nature that had a tendency to go out of control. If you allow your mind or your flesh to do anything, it will! The Bible teaches us that there is no good thing in the flesh.

> *For I know that in me (that is, in my flesh,) dwelleth no good thing...*
>
> **Romans 7:18**

There is no good thing in your fleshly nature. Do not give it an opportunity to go out of bounds.

> ... make not provision for the flesh, to fulfil the lusts thereof.
>
> **Romans 13:14**

Dreams from the Devil

As usual, the devil has a counterfeit for everything that God does. Satan's specialty is to deceive and to trick.

God is not the author of confusion. **A dream, which brings confusion, is not from God.** The Spirit of God is not a spirit of fear. Something that comes to frighten you is not from the Spirit of the Lord.

Many people have been snared by the devil through dreams. Satan will give you a picture of some evil event and tell you that the dream is going to happen. The devil may show you a picture of your coffin and your funeral. Many Christians have been trapped into disasters, untimely deaths and all manner of wickedness by demonic dreams.

How People Are Trapped by Demonic Dreams

People are trapped into childlessness and barrenness by means of dreams. This is how it happens: Satan shows them a picture of barrenness or a picture of them sleeping with someone else. These dreams have one aim: to frighten you and to instil fear into your heart.

> *Then thou SCAREST me with dreams, and TERRIFIEST me through visions:*
>
> **Job 7:14**

You begin to fear that you will not have a child. You begin to fear that things will not work out normally for you. After all, your dreams show you unknown people sleeping with you! When fear has taken a foothold, the real thing can happen! Fear is not a mood or a feeling; it is a demonic spirit.

> *For God hath not given us the spirit of fear...*
>
> **2 Timothy 1:7**

Remember that Job eventually experienced what he was afraid of. God had blessed him. God had given him houses, lands, prosperity, children and great riches. Yet, he was afraid that something bad could happen to him. Eventually, his fears came to pass.

> *For the thing which I greatly feared is come upon me, and that which I was afraid of is come unto me.*
>
> **Job 3:25**

Be careful of the things that you fear because the things that you fear will happen! That is why Jesus often said, "FEAR NOT! Only believe!"

Many years ago, when I was living with my parents, thieves invaded our home. I happened to wake up in the night at about 3:00 a.m. and I heard some noise downstairs. A gang of thieves had broken into our house and were carrying away everything that they could. I shouted, waking up the entire neighbourhood, but the thieves escaped in a get-away car!

Later on, I discovered how the thieves were able to get into the house. They had removed two louvre blades from the window and helped one of their gang members to enter the house. It must have been a very small individual because the space created was very small. **This person who entered the house then opened the main doors and let the rest of the robbers (demons) in.**

This is how the devil works. He just needs to get one member of his team into your mind. That one spirit will open the door for many other demons to enter.

When fear is allowed to take a foothold in your life, it opens the door to destruction, untimely death, sickness and barrenness. Job said that he was frightened by dreams. God will not send you a spirit of fear. Later on when these frightening dreams occur people say, "You see, it has happened just as I dreamt." No! **It has happened just as you feared!**

Chapter 18

How to Relate to a Prophet

There are many people who feel that they must be led by a personal prophecy coming from a prophet. I personally know of many Christians who have made major changes in their lives because of something a prophet told them. Is this scriptural?

In this chapter, I want to share with you about what I believe is the proper role of a prophet in the Church. You must know what a prophet is supposed to do; otherwise, you may find your life destroyed by someone claiming to be a prophet.

> ... O my people, they which lead thee cause thee to err, and destroy the way of thy paths.
>
> **Isaiah 3:12**

Are our lives supposed to be guided by prophets? The answer is NO! As New Testament believers we are supposed to be guided by the Holy Spirit and the Word of God.

> *For as many as are led by the Spirit of God, they are the sons of God.*
>
> **Romans 8:14**

The role that the prophets of the Old Testament played was different from that of New Testament prophets. Am I saying that New Testament prophets did not have the power to see visions and receive "words" from the Lord? They certainly did have this power but it operated within a different context.

Under the Old Covenant, only the prophet and perhaps the priest had the Holy Spirit working through them. Today, the Holy Spirit is in every believer and is giving us personal guidance on a day-to-day basis. **We still need the input of prophets, but we do not need to seek them for daily guidance.** We also need to check whatever they say, to see whether it agrees with what the Holy Spirit is telling us.

> *Let the prophets speak two or three, and let the other judge.*
>
> **1 Corinthians 14:29**

Under the New Testament, the declarations of prophets are supposed to be judged or assessed. How can we judge what the prophet says if we don't have the Holy Spirit or the Word? The Word of God provides a standard by which we can assess what is happening.

For instance, I have noticed how many prophets minister in churches, giving personal prophecies to individuals. I have watched prophets telling members of one particular church that the Lord wants them to move out of that church into the church that he, the prophet, is establishing.

There are prophets who have destabilized entire churches with this type of message. I know a church that lost about five hundred members through the ministry of one such prophet. This same visiting prophet gave a prophecy to the associate pastor of the church, telling him that the Lord wanted him to move on. The next thing we discovered was that this associate pastor had become a resident pastor in the prophet's new church.

If I were to judge such an action by the Word of God, I would quote to you from the book of Ephesians. Paul shows us the role of apostles, prophets, evangelists, pastors and teachers. They are to minister to the Body of Christ so that the saints become stable Christians. Read it for yourself:

> *And he gave some, apostles; and some, prophets…*
> *That we henceforth be no more children, tossed to and*
> *fro, and carried about…*
>
> **Ephesians 4:11, 14**

If a true prophet comes to minister in your church, you will know him by his fruits. If the fruit (the end result) of his ministry were destabilization and a moving of church members to and fro, I would wonder whether he's a New Testament prophet. Read it for yourself! Prophets are supposed to minister and prevent the to and fro movement of church members. They are supposed to prevent them from being carried about by every new idea.

I would not advise any pastor to welcome a so-called prophet to destabilize the church that he has taken years to build. As a pastor, my duty is to gather sheep. My call is to prevent them from being lost. **I want to be able to say to Jesus, "Of all that you have given me, I have lost none."** I believe that I am a good pastor so I will fight for every single sheep that God has assigned to me.

The Reaping Prophet

I remember having a discussion with a certain prophet. This prophet had ministered privately to several prominent church members of mine, telling them that the Lord wanted them to move out of my church. The prophet did not know that I knew about these different destabilizing "prophecies" he had given to my people. In fact, as at the time we were speaking, some of my church members had become members of his church.

I asked him, "How is the ministry?"

He said, "It's doing well. I have had a few problems but I am surviving."

We got to discuss other things. Then he told me, "You know, I invited a prophet to minister in my church." (Although he was a prophet, he was pastoring a church.)

He continued, "This prophet really did me in."

"What do you mean?" I asked.

"I invited him to minister in my church and he began to prophesy to all my members and directed them to see him privately," he explained.

He lamented, "By the time this prophet had finished the convention, I had lost a large section of my church to him. This prophet gave accurate prophecies, and after the faith of the people was lifted, he told them that God wanted them to leave their church."

I listened quietly as the prophet/pastor spoke of his experience.

"He has met his match," I thought to myself. "Perhaps he has forgotten similar prophecies which he gave to my church members!"

This prophet did not know that he was reaping the destabilization he had sown in other people's churches.

You do not need a prophet to tell you which church to attend. You do not need a prophet to tell you whom to marry. You do not need a prophet to tell you to give away your car or your life's savings. You have the Word of God! You have the Holy Spirit and you have your common sense that we spoke about in an earlier chapter.

The Bible tells us that God speaks to us in the New Testament, mainly by His Word and not by His prophets.

> *God, who at sundry times and in divers manners spake in time past unto the fathers by the prophets, Hath in these last days spoken unto us by his Son [the Word]...*
>
> **Hebrews 1:1, 2**

Do not allow any so-called prophet to rob you of your possessions. The accuracy of prophecies can be so frightening that you will feel that God must be speaking. Sometimes, some prophets have an evil spirit operating through them. They give accurate "words of knowledge" by satanic power and then they rob you of your money.

There are also some prophets who operate by a mixture of spirits. They will minister very accurately by the Spirit of God. After realizing how enchanted you are by the accuracy of the gift, they will move into the flesh and operate by another spirit. Is it possible for someone to operate with two different spirits at the same time? Of course it is! Samson had the Spirit of God operating in him, whilst at the same time he was operating in a spirit of adultery and fornication.

Remember when Jesus asked Peter, "Who do men say that I am?" Peter answered accurately. Jesus immediately confirmed that Peter was moving in the Holy Spirit. There was no way Peter could have known what he knew, except the Spirit of God had revealed it to him. However, in the discussion that followed, Peter began to speak as inspired by Satan and Jesus had to rebuke him saying, "Satan, get thee behind me." Watch Peter under the influence of the Holy Spirit.

> *He saith unto them, But whom say ye that I am? And Simon Peter answered and said, Thou art the Christ,*

the Son of the living God. And Jesus answered and said unto him, Blessed art thou, Simon Barjona: for flesh and blood hath not revealed it unto thee, but my Father which is in heaven.

Matthew 16:15-17

Now watch Peter under the influence of Satan.

From that time forth began Jesus to shew unto his disciples, how that he must go unto Jerusalem, and suffer many things of the elders and chief priests and scribes, and be killed, and be raised again the third day. Then Peter took him, and began to rebuke him, saying, Be it far from thee, Lord: this shall not be unto thee. But he turned, and said unto Peter, Get thee behind me, Satan: THOU ART AN OFFENSE UNTO ME: for thou savourest not the things that be of God, but those that be of men.

Matthew 16:21-23

How to Relate with a Real Prophet

So what exactly is a prophet supposed to do? How should I relate to someone who calls himself a prophet? Let us study the ministry of Jesus since He was a great prophet. Each office of the Body of Christ: apostle, prophet, evangelist, pastor and teacher, has several different ministries under it. A prophet will also have different ministries operating under his office.

A minister who stands in the office of a prophet will primarily function in the ministry of preaching and teaching. Beware of so-called prophets who do not preach the Word of God but *only* give personal prophecies. Don't misunderstand me, I believe in personal prophecies.

However, let it be very clear that anything that does not put the Word of God in its proper place is doomed to failure with the passage of time. "In the beginning was the *Word*..." "Let the *Word* of Christ dwell in you richly..." "Thy *Word* is a light unto my path... The entrance of thy *Word* giveth light..." Anything without the *Word* is in darkness and is not of God.

All offices of the ministry have a primary function of teaching and preaching. The Word comes first and is of paramount importance in every ministerial office. After preaching and teaching the Word, a prophet may operate in the ministry of healing, and other revelation gifts like the "word of knowledge" and "word of wisdom". The prophet may also flow in the ministry of predictive prophecy or exhortative prophecy. From Scripture, you will see that Jesus was a great prophet.

> *... and they glorified God, saying, That a great prophet is risen up among us...*
>
> **Luke 7:16**

But His principal ministry was to go about preaching and teaching the Word of God.

> *And Jesus went about all the cities and villages, teaching in their synagogues, and preaching the gospel...*
>
> **Matthew 9:35**

Jesus had a healing ministry.

> *How God anointed Jesus... who went about doing good, and healing all that were oppressed of the devil...*
>
> **Acts 10:38**

He also operated in the gifts of revelation. Standing in the office of a prophet, He ministered to the woman of Samaria:

> *For thou hast had five husbands; and he whom thou now hast is not thy husband...*
>
> **John 4:18**

The woman of Samaria immediately realized that she had met someone standing in the office of a prophet. Look at her response to Jesus' ministration.

> *The woman saith unto him, Sir, I perceive that thou art a prophet.*
>
> **John 4:19**

Jesus also operated in the ministry of predictive prophecy. In the book of Matthew, Chapter 24, He predicted the destruction of Solomon's temple. This happened in AD 70 when the Romans destroyed Jerusalem.

Speaking of the temple He said:

> ... There shall not be left here one stone upon another...
>
> **Matthew 24:2**

Jesus gave extensive predictions concerning the end of the world. We would do well to take note of these prophecies because Jesus was a great prophet.

The Ministry of a Prophet

It is clear from the above account that a prophet is someone who *preaches* and *teaches*. He also ministers *healing* and operates in the *word of knowledge*. A prophet also gives predictive and exhortative *prophecies.* This is a complete prophetic ministry, and as you can see, the Word of God comes first. Look out for real prophets and stay with what is authentic. Look for proven prophets whose foundation is the Word of God. That is how to relate to your prophet.

Chapter 19

The Secret of Directed Paths

Trust in the LORD with all thine heart; and lean not unto thine own understanding. In all thy ways acknowledge him, and he shall direct thy paths.

Proverbs 3:5, 6

God leads us through directed paths. The promise of God in this Scripture is not that God will direct you! God is promising here that He will direct your paths. What is the difference between God directing you and God directing your paths? When God directs you, He speaks to you and tells you what to do. It is then up to you to do the right thing and obey His voice. However, when God directs your paths, *you* don't have to do anything. It is your paths that have to obey instructions.

Your duty is to trust the Lord that He has arranged the circumstances so that you will naturally flow into His will. This is what happens when you pray, "Thy will be done." Jesus prayed "Thy will be done" for three hours in the Garden of Gethsemane. After getting an answer to that prayer, Jesus didn't have to do anything any more. He just allowed things to happen naturally.

God Ignores You and Speaks to Your Paths

Once I was walking in a major international airport. Those of you who have travelled a bit know that modern airports are monstrous buildings with an often intricate maze of tunnels and corridors. This was the first time I had been in that particular airport. I travel frequently so I know my way around many major airports. This time however, I did not know the way. When I got out of the plane I just kept walking. As I walked in that airport, God gave me a revelation.

I didn't get lost at all, not even for one minute! I walked confidently through the labyrinth of airport corridors and arrived at the right place to pick up my baggage. Would you believe that no one told me where to go or what to do, but I just kept walking?

God showed me that I did not get lost in that airport because the authorities had arranged the corridors and tunnels in such a way that I could only go in one direction and arrive in one particular place.

As I walked through the airport, I realized that many doors were shut. Access to many parts of the airport was blocked to me. There were signs everywhere showing where newly arrived passengers should go.

That is often how God will lead you if you will take the time to pray that His will be done in your life. Then you can walk on confidently. **You may not even know what exactly to do, but as you keep on praying that His will be done, He will direct your paths.** God will block certain doors and make it impossible for you to go on certain roads.

He will ensure that you will only flow in a particular direction. He will ensure that you only meet certain people.

There are many times I don't know what to do. I am not a superman. I cannot pretend to know the mind of God all the time. Nobody knows all the will of God. Even Jesus prayed that the will of God be done. I spend hours praying that the will of God be done in my life. I believe that every serious Christian should do that!

If you have committed your way to God, as the Bible says in Proverbs 3:5 and 6, God is committed to directing the paths of your life.

Do not cry any more because that man did not marry you. Do not be sad because that opportunity did not work out. Did you not pray that the will of God should be done? Did you not commit your ways to Him? God is answering your prayers right now! He is directing your life. You do not have to hear a voice. You do not need to see a vision. Just continue walking by faith and you will find yourself in His perfect will.

Chapter 20

How to Deal with the Voice of the People

Another important area of influence is the voice of human beings. What others say and do influences many people. Most of the time we want to be like others. Whatever the people in your peer group are doing is what you want to do! But many times that is not the will of God.

God created a special nation called Israel. He planned to rule the nation directly through His prophets and spiritual leaders. When the people of Israel realized that all the nations around them had kings, they also decided to have a king. Even though what they were experiencing was better, they just wanted to follow the crowd.

> Then all the elders of Israel gathered themselves together, and came to Samuel unto Ramah, And said unto him, Behold, thou art old, and thy sons walk not in thy ways: NOW MAKE US A KING TO JUDGE US LIKE ALL THE NATIONS. And the LORD said unto Samuel, Hearken unto the voice of the people in

> *all that they say unto thee: for they have not rejected thee, but they have rejected me, that I should not reign over them... howbeit yet protest solemnly unto them... Nevertheless the people refused to obey the voice of Samuel; and they said, NAY; BUT WE WILL HAVE A KING OVER US; THAT WE ALSO MAY BE LIKE ALL THE NATIONS...*
>
> **1 Samuel 8:4, 5, 7, 9, 19, 20**

That is what I call "the voice of the people". It is such a strong voice that it often drowns out the gentle voice of the Holy Spirit. You must be careful not to become someone who is easily affected by the opinions of those around. No one can be a successful minister if he still wants to please people around. That is why a church must not be run by democracy. The essential nature of democracy turns people into men-pleasers and liars.

> *... for if I yet pleased men, I should not be the servant of Christ.*
>
> **Galatians 1:10**

If you want to serve the Lord, you must be careful not to become a man-pleaser. I am wary of people who are very conscious of making good impressions everywhere. Such people are usually two-faced and can easily betray you.

On the 10th of March 1989, I qualified as a medical doctor. I was pastoring this fledgling church along with some other medical colleagues of mine. As was the custom, after one year of working in the hospital, most of my colleagues left the country for the USA and England. They were going to do further studies and earn more money.

At that time, I came under a lot of pressure from family and friends. They said, "You are a doctor. You have a bright future before you." My father wanted me to specialize at the Cambridge University but I knew that the Lord had called me and I could not leave the ministry. My father-in-law even offered to help get me into a good department of the Teaching Hospital.

I always noticed the anxious and questioning look of my mother-in-law. My mother-in-law is very sweet and really cared about us. She was worried about both her daughter and me. I'm sure she thought I was destroying my life by refusing to pursue a lucrative and dignified medical career. One day the pressure was so much, I had to tell my dear concerned mother-in-law not to bring up the topic anymore.

At that time, our church was an unimpressive group of students and struggling Christians. A pastor's job has always been a controversial and disrespected profession. My father said to me, "What sort of job is this that pays by the collection of people's pennies? That is not an honourable way to live!"

I was under a lot of pressure. If I had yielded to the pressure of the people, perhaps all the souls who have been saved through this ministry would have perished. I am sure that there are people who are not in the ministry today because they listened to the voice of the people.

I have decided to ignore the voice of the people when I am sure that God wants me to do something. I may look controversial! I may displease people! But I am accountable to God for my calling. Woe is me if I preach not the Gospel!

People around say, "Do this" or "Do that"! They say to me, "You must have a hospital." Others tell me, "You must have a university!" Still others say, "You must travel more often to other churches." But what does God say?

Does God want me to use a million dollars to build a hospital or does He want me to use a million dollars to plant churches? I intend to do His will. You ensure that you do His will for your life and I'll make sure that I'm doing His will for mine! **The voice of the people is the voice that drowns the voice of the Holy Spirit.**

There are many ladies who yield to the voice of the people. "Why are you a virgin at this age? Enjoy yourself and have some fun!" They will put pressure on you to marry an unbeliever. "He's a good guy. If you marry him you will be happy." But the silent voice of the Word of God tells you not to be unequally yoked with unbelievers.

I know some associate pastors who are told by the congregation members, "You are a great pastor. I only enjoy coming to church when you are preaching." The voice of the people is telling them, "If you were your own boss and not an assistant, you would do very well in ministry." Perhaps they would do very well in ministry. Perhaps God is calling them to a great new work. **But make sure that it is the voice of the Holy Spirit that you follow and not the voice of the people.**

Some Jezebel-like wives tell their husbands, "You could have a nice car and a lot of money if you broke away from this tyrant of a General Overseer." "Come on," they say, "Do your own thing!" The voice of a wife is a very strong voice. It takes a very principled man to stay on course when his wife is prodding him to flow in another direction.

Never forget this! The voice of the people is the voice that drowns the voice of the Holy Spirit. It was not they who called you into the ministry! People cannot bless you! People cannot promote you! If you follow what people say, you will have to look to people for promotion. **But promotion does not come from people, it comes from the Lord.**

> *For promotion cometh neither from the east, nor from the west, nor from the south. But God is the judge: he putteth down one, and setteth up another.*
>
> **Psalm 75:6, 7**

Not only are people powerless to help you, but they often turn against you after a while. Do you remember how people hailed Jesus as the Messiah on Palm Sunday? Just a few days later the same people screamed, "Crucify Him!" The people who hailed Him did a one hundred and eighty degree turnaround and murdered Him.

Do not let the voice of friends or family come up higher than the voice of the Spirit of God.

Chapter 21

How Not to Be Led by Circumstances

> *... and the care of this world, and the deceitfulness of riches, choke the word, and he becometh unfruitful.*
> **Matthew 13:22**

The word circumstance is self-explanatory. "Circum" speaks of things around and "stances" speaks of things standing. **Therefore, "circumstances" simply mean "things standing around in your life".** These circumstances could be school, marriage, work or any situational factors.

Circumstances often dictate what Christians should do. **We are to be led by the Spirit of God and not by circumstances.** You cannot allow the circumstances in your life to prevent you from doing what you must do.

When I became a medical student, I had very little time to do the work of God. The circumstances were such that it was almost impossible for me to pray or read my Bible. But what was the silent voice of the Word of God telling me? The Word of God was telling me to be steadfast, unmovable and always abounding in the work of the Lord.

> *Therefore, my beloved brethren, BE YE STEDFAST, UNMOVEABLE, ALWAYS ABOUNDING in the work of the Lord, forasmuch as ye know that your labour is not in vain in the Lord.*
> **1 Corinthians 15:58**

And that is exactly what I did. The circumstances of a medical student were well known to other students. Because of this, medical students were not allowed to be leaders of the Christian fellowship. They knew that the circumstances of a medical student's life did not allow for much spiritual activity.

You see, we were picked up by a bus at 7a.m. everyday and shuttled to the Teaching Hospital, about an hour's drive away. We stayed there all day until the evening. When we returned to the university campus at about 6:00 p.m., we were exhausted and had a lot of academic work to do.

How on earth could one be a useful Christian leader and at the same time pass the medical exams? But the good news is that I was able to do it by the grace of God. In my first year, I started a Christian ministry on the university campus. That ministry is still there today! During my fourth year, I established a church that has grown into a worldwide ministry.

There are many Christians who are led by circumstances. That is why they fall away from the Lord. The cares of this world (circumstances) quench the call!

> *... and the care of this world, and the deceitfulness of riches, choke the word, and he becometh unfruitful.*
>
> **Matthew 13:22**

God calls many people. However, the call of many is quenched by the circumstances of life. Many people are unfruitful today not because they are evil. **They are unfruitful because the voice of circumstances prevailed over the voice of the Spirit.**

When you have a baby, you are saddled with a real stressful schedule. It is up to you to rise above the circumstances and pray. Are you telling me that having a baby is a curse? Are you telling me that being married is a curse? If it is not a curse to you why do you allow these new circumstances to quench the zeal you once had? Rise up today in the name of Jesus. Rise above the voice of your circumstances.

God has called you to do great things in this life. **It is only great men who rise above the voice of circumstances.**

Chapter 22

How to Unmask the Devil

And the devil said unto him...

Luke 4:3

Our Lord Jesus was spoken to by the devil. Satan spoke to Him about three different topics. If you think that Satan will never speak to you, then you are joking. The devil tempts and tests everyone.

Jesus taught, "A servant is not above his master." If He was tempted, then we will also be tempted. It is easy to summarize the works of the devil into one word – *deception*. The devil is a liar and a deceiver. Jesus called him the father of liars.

> *Ye are of your father the devil, and the lusts of your father ye will do. He was a murderer from the beginning, and abode not in the truth, because there is no truth in him. When he speaketh a lie, he speaketh of his own: for he is a liar, and the father of it.*
>
> **John 8:44**

The Bible describes Satan as someone who deceives the whole world. Anyone who can deceive the entire world must be a very good liar and deceiver.

> ... that old serpent, called the Devil, and Satan, which deceiveth the whole world...
>
> **Revelation 12:9**

I know some politicians who have been able to deceive the masses. Some of them are able to deceive tribes and regions of a country. But to deceive the whole world is an awesome achievement. This means that all the intelligent and wise people have been taken in by the lie.

If you visit Europe today, you will see millions of people who believe that there is no God. They sincerely think that religion is not practical. They believe that life is all on this earth and that when you die you are dead like a dog. It is not a few people who hold this concept. These ideas are held by multitudes of intelligent but deceived Europeans.

Satan has managed to captivate the minds and hearts of this world with gold, silver and pleasure. Even when the realities of death and life dawn on people at funerals, the intellectuals of this world still refuse to acknowledge the existence of God.

Satan will produce a counterfeit to anything that God does in an attempt to deceive us. If the Holy Spirit gives dreams, Satan will also come up with his own dreams. If God speaks in an audible voice, Satan will also give audible voices to confuse and deceive you. That is why the Bible says there are many voices in the world and none of them is without signification.

> *There are, it may be, so many kinds of voices in the world, and none of them is without signification.*
>
> **1 Corinthians 14:10**

The devil may open doors to deceive you. Satan also tries to close certain doors in your life. That is why Jesus is described as the one who can open the door that no one can ever close. That is what distinguishes the opening of a door by Jesus and the opening of a door by someone else.

> *... he that openeth, and no man shutteth; and shutteth, and no man openeth;*
>
> **Revelation 3:7**

If God has opened a door for you to marry Araba-Lucy, you will marry her. Nothing can stop it and nothing can change it! If God has determined that you should be a pastor over thousands of people, the wicked lies of your detractors cannot close that open door. If God has determined that you should be a millionaire in His kingdom, the economic circumstances around will not stop the blessings of God.

Our main job is to be able to decipher the deceptive traps and lies of the enemy. The Bible never teaches that we should beware of the power of the devil. Satan's strength is not in his power. In fact, he is powerless against you.

That is why God's instruction to us is to be careful of his tricks and lying traps.

Put on the whole armour of God, that ye may be able to stand against the wiles [deception, tricks, lies] of the devil.

Ephesians 6:11

Chapter 23

Three Checks to Avoiding Mistakes When Being Led by the Spirit

How do we fight against lying voices? There are three safety checks you must adhere to. This is to rule out the possibility of listening to the wrong voice.

Rule out the possibility of following the voice of your flesh by being honest with yourself. Admit to yourself when you realize that your flesh is influencing you. Remember that to be carnally minded is death.

Three Important Safety Checks

1. The safety of a multitude of counsellors

> *... in the multitude of counsellors there is safety.*
>
> **Proverbs 11:14**

There is nothing like the safety of counselling. If you have had a revelation from God, subject it to many counsellors (there is a difference between a counsellor and a friend). When you subject your revelations to a multitude of counsellors, you expose yourself to more information that helps you to take better decisions.

One aspiring pastor wanted to marry a young lady in the church. He prayed for several hours about whom he should marry. He finally came up with a decision and said that God had told him to marry a certain lady. Just before he proposed to the young lady, he decided to consult with an elder and with his pastor.

The elder said to him, "She's a nice girl. I see nothing wrong with your entering a relationship with this Christian lady."

Then, as a matter of formality, he decided to mention it to his pastor. When he did, the pastor said, "Oh, I see. She is a nice lady; however, I want you to be aware of one important thing." He told the aspiring suitor, "This young lady has a severe mental disease. I prayed for her myself when she developed the condition."

The pastor went on, "As far as I know, she is still taking medication to control the effects of this condition."

He continued, "Of course, this does not bar you from marrying her. However, it is important for you to be aware of this reality before you take a decision."

The young man was taken aback, "Oh, I didn't know this!" he exclaimed.

He told the pastor, "Thank you very much. It will help me to take an informed decision."

This young man's safety depended on his consulting with more than one counsellor. The first counsellor (the elder) had nothing contrary to say. It was the second counsellor (the pastor) who had very important facts that the man needed to know.

You can see from this true-life story that the safety of this young man lay in the *multitude* of counsellors. There is no revelation, voice or instruction from God that cannot be subjected to a multitude of counsellors.

This is the reason why married couples must undergo extensive counselling. Many people who are getting married don't know the realities that are ahead of them. They have no idea about the journey that they are about to undertake. Their safety lies in the multitude of counsellors.

2. Prove all things

Prove all things; hold fast that which is good.
1 Thessalonians 5:21

Has a prophet spoken to you? Have you received a personal prophecy? Have you heard a voice from God? Please subject it to the test of the Word of God. Please prove all voices that you claim to have heard from God.

I sometimes operate in the prophetic gift. When I have a word of knowledge about someone, I often ask the individual concerned about the word I have received. I want to see if it is true and accurate because I know that I could be wrong. When a so-called prophet gives you a word of knowledge to leave your husband for another, please submit it to the Word of God.

Is it not the Word of God that tells us not to divorce? How could it be that a prophetic voice is speaking contrary to the Word of God?

Prophets Can Make Mistakes

A prophet prophesied to two of my leaders who were about to become pastors. He told them that within a year they would be living outside Ghana. He went on to tell them that they would be in the ministry but it would not be under the banner of Lighthouse Chapel International. These pastors were confused and wondered whether the Lord had spoken or not!

A year passed and these pastors were no nearer to going abroad than I was to the moon. After two years, it was quite clear that this prophecy had not materialized.

They have rather become pastors who are established in Lighthouse Chapel International in Ghana. The passage of time proved that this was either a mistaken prophet or a mistaken prophecy. Prophets are human, and they also make mistakes.

> *But the prophet, which shall presume to speak a word in my name, WHICH I HAVE NOT COMMANDED HIM TO SPEAK, or that shall speak in the name of*

> *other gods, even that prophet shall die. When a prophet speaketh in the name of the LORD, if the thing follow not, nor come to pass, that is the thing which the LORD hath not spoken, but THE PROPHET HATH SPOKEN IT PRESUMPTUOUSLY: thou shalt not be afraid of him.*
>
> **Deuteronomy 18:20, 22**

***All* prophets, prophecies, revelations and voices must be proved.** We must hold on to what is good. If you swallow every prophecy, revelation and dream hook, line and sinker, you will soon find yourself gobbling down garbage.

When Paul received the call and revelation from God, he subjected it to a valid test. Paul had more revelations than any of the prophets we have around today, but notice how he practised this safety principle.

> *But when it pleased God, who separated me from my mother's womb, and called me by his grace, To reveal his Son in me, that I might preach him among the heathen; immediately I conferred not with flesh and blood: Neither went I up to Jerusalem to them which were apostles before me; but I went into Arabia, and returned again unto Damascus.*
>
> **Galatians 1:15-17**

Paul received a revelation from God. He did not confer with flesh and blood. The revelation was directly from the Lord. But after several years, look at how Paul subjected his revelation to the scrutiny of senior apostles. If you don't want trouble, follow the principles that Paul practised and you will experience a sound and balanced ministry.

> *Then fourteen years after I went up again to Jerusalem with Barnabas, and took Titus with me also. And I went up by revelation, AND COMMUNICATED UNTO THEM THAT GOSPEL WHICH I PREACH AMONG THE GENTILES, BUT PRIVATELY TO THEM WHICH WERE OF REPUTATION, LEST BY ANY MEANS I SHOULD RUN, OR HAD RUN, IN VAIN.*
>
> **Galatians 2:1, 2**

Paul received a revelation from God in Arabia. But he subjected his revelation to the scrutiny of Peter and other apostles who were of reputation. This is your key to safety in a minefield where there are many dangerous voices.

3. The confirmation of two witnesses

> *… In the mouth of two or three witnesses shall every word be established.*
>
> **2 Corinthians 13:1**

God has set a standard in His Word. It says that the mouth of two or more witnesses establishes a thing. **God's safety rule is simple: do not accept it unless a second witness confirms it.**

If a prophet gives a "word", you may ask, "Who is the second witness?" **The second witness can be you.** The prophecy can confirm something that God has already spoken to you about.

Even when it comes to dreams, a second dream helps to confirm the message that came in the first dream. Notice how Joseph applied this principle when he was interpreting dreams for Pharaoh.

> *And for that the dream was doubled unto Pharaoh twice; it is because the thing is established by God, and God will shortly bring it to pass.*
>
> **Genesis 41:32**

The principle of confirmation by two witnesses is an important safety check for everyone who desires to safely experience the voice of God's direction for his life.

Chapter 24

Why You Must Listen to Your Conscience

God has given everybody a conscience. The conscience is that quiet inner voice that checks us when we go wrong. In charismatic circles, we hardly hear anything about the conscience. Your conscience is that quiet voice within that tells you when you are doing something wrong.

There are times when your heart (spirit) condemns you for doing something wrong.

> *For if OUR HEART CONDEMN US, God is greater than our heart, and knoweth all things. Beloved, if our heart condemn us not, then have we confidence toward God.*
>
> **1 John 3:20, 21**

Your heart has the ability to condemn you for wrongdoing. It is only when your heart is not condemning you that you have confidence to approach God. The confidence comes because you know that you are doing the right thing. Pastors will do well to follow their consciences in the ministry. Christians will do well to follow the voice of their conscience. Apostle Paul said that he always tried to maintain a good conscience.

> *And herein do I exercise myself, to have always a CONSCIENCE VOID OF OFFENCE toward God, and toward men.*
>
> **Acts 24:16**

Any Christian who decides to follow his conscience will end up being a moral and upright person before the Lord. David prayed that God should keep him in the path of righteousness. **Your conscience is the instrument by which God will keep you in the path of righteousness.** Anyone who claims to be led by the Spirit or by prophets, but does not listen to the voice of his conscience is doomed to tragedy in life and ministry.

As you continue to ignore the voice of your conscience, it becomes deadened and hardened. This is what Paul described as having your conscience seared.

> *Speaking lies in hypocrisy; having their CONSCIENCE SEARED with a hot iron;*
>
> **1 Timothy 4:2**

One minister was having an affair with one of his members. The lady asked him, "Pastor, how will you be able to preach tomorrow?" He laughed and said, "Oh, when I commit fornication I feel the anointing flowing even more."

This minister was used to committing immoral sins. It was now part and parcel of his life and ministry. *His conscience was no longer condemning him.* His conscience had become hardened. He now thought that sin was funny and made jokes about how the anointing was enhanced by fornication.

As soon as you make a mistake, respond to the voice of your heart condemning you. It will cause you to repent and get in line. After some years of neglecting your conscience, you will make shipwreck of your ministry. Shipwreck simply means disaster!

> *Holding faith, and a good conscience; which SOME HAVING PUT AWAY concerning faith have made SHIPWRECK:*
>
> **1 Timothy 1:19**

I have watched ministers who ignored their consciences. The end of such ministries is one and the same – shipwreck! This is why you must be careful about the thoughts you allow into your mind. If you permit certain thoughts, they will lead to other developments. **This is why you must be careful about telling lies, however small they are.**

Keep your conscience clear! Let your heart prick you whenever you are wrong! The voice of your conscience will lead you safely on the path of righteousness. I pray for you that you will live this life with the benefit of God's direction. I see you enjoying divine guidance as you apply the principles in this book to your everyday life!

Chapter 25

Twelve Levels of Obedience to the Lord

… no king since the time of Josiah has approached HIS RECORD OF OBEDIENCE.
2 Kings 23:25 (TLB)

A quick study will reveal different levels of obedience when it comes to following the voice of God and the voice of the Holy Spirit. This is because there are different kinds of instructions that God gives. Indeed, there are different types of commandments. Jesus, speaking of one of God's commandments said: this command is like the other commandment. "This is the first and great commandment… and the second is like unto it." (Matthew 22:38-39).

Some of the instructions are hard and difficult and some are nice and easy. Some are so hard and so difficult that few people ever obey them. Others are so nice and so easy that people cannot believe that God is the one behind those commands. Amazingly, all these different instructions of the Lord give rise to different levels of response that I call the "levels of obedience".

Would you obey the Lord if He asked you to give someone food?

Would you obey the Lord if He asked you to live until you were ninety?

Would you obey the Lord if He asked you to live for only thirty years?

Jesus Christ obeyed everything He was asked to do and He is our best example of someone who obeyed God at all levels. I want you to look at the different levels of obedience and see where you fit in. What is your record of obedience?

Are you ready to follow the Holy Spirit in the journey of life?

1. The first level of obedience is: obeying instructions that are pleasurable.

For instance, most husbands are happy and excited to obey the scriptural command to have sex with their wives. No discipline and no counsel is needed to get many husbands to obey this instruction. That is why it is the first level of obedience.

> *The husband should not deprive his wife of sexual intimacy, which is her right as a married woman, nor should the wife deprive her husband.*
>
> **1 Corinthians 7:3, (NLT)**

2. The second level of obedience is: obeying instructions that are in tandem with your personal goals and childhood dreams.

God tells us to do many things including those that are in line with our childhood dreams. Those instructions are also easy to follow. Take for instance the message of "wisdom" which teaches us to "seek wisdom, for length of days is in her right hand; and in her left hand riches and honour" (Proverbs 3:16).

This is a very "likeable" commandment from the Lord because we all want long life, riches and honour. We understand these instructions and we love them because we see how they will take us to the top.

Today, churches are filled with success-oriented and prosperity-loving congregants who are delighted that their pastors' sermons coincide exactly with these personal needs and dreams.

Indeed, churches get larger and larger as the pastors continue to feed the congregations with exactly what they want to hear. Pastors are under pressure to preach what the people want to hear rather than what the Lord wants to tell them. It is no wonder that most pastors have become experts at delivering beautiful sermons on financial wisdom, money, success in life, marriage, family happiness, abundance and prosperity.

Many people go to church on Sunday morning for the pastor to scratch them on the exact spot that is itching.

When Jesus gave out bread and fish, the crowds multiplied. But when He told them the hard truth of eating His flesh and drinking His blood, the crowds whittled down to twelve men.

People love instructions that coincide with their personal goals and childhood dreams.

3. The third level obedience is: obeying instructions that are reasonable.

Many of God's commands are reasonable and easy to understand. The commandment, "Do not steal" is reasonable. Everyone can see that this command will keep you out of prison and out of trouble. The Word of God commands Christians not to steal and urges them to work hard. "Let him that stole steal no more: but rather let him labour, working with his hands the thing which is good, that he may have to give to him that needeth" (Ephesians 4:28). This is the third level of obedience: obeying instructions that are reasonable and sensible!

4. The fourth level of obedience is: obeying instructions that lead to something good for you.

Once again, there are instructions that clearly lead to a better life for you. These are instructions that Christians easily embrace. For instance, the instruction, "Honour thy father and mother; ... that it may be well with thee, and thou mayest live long on the earth" (Ephesians 6:2-3).

I want it to be well with me and I want to live long! Everybody can say that. This is an instruction that everyone understands will lead to something good.

5. The fifth level of obedience is: obeying instructions when you know why the instructions have been given.

Sometimes God gives us instructions and helps us to understand why He is commanding us. For instance, Jesus said,

> *But I say unto you, Love your enemies, bless them that curse you, do good to them that hate you, and pray for them which despitefully use you, and persecute you;*
>
> *That ye may be the children of your Father which is in heaven: for he maketh his sun to rise on the evil and on the good, and sendeth rain on the just and on the unjust.*
>
> *For if ye love them which love you, what reward have ye? do not even the publicans the same?*
>
> *And if ye salute your brethren only, what do ye more than others? do not even the publicans so?*
>
> *Be ye therefore PERFECT, even as your Father which is in heaven is perfect.*
>
> **Matthew 5:44-48**

He gave this instruction because He wanted us to be perfect just like our heavenly Father. He told us how we can become perfect like our heavenly Father. From this Scripture we can all see *why* God is giving us this instruction.

6. The sixth level of obedience is: obeying instructions that you do not understand.

> *... every where and in all things I am instructed both to be full and to be hungry, both to abound and to suffer need.*
>
> **Philippians 4:12**

Paul said he had been instructed to be hungry and to be full.

Why would he have these completely conflicting instructions?

What is the benefit of being hungry?

Why should I suffer need? How does that help anybody?

I do not understand how being hungry and suffering need helps the ministry. But there are instructions that God gives that you will never understand. It takes a higher level of obedience to obey instructions that you do not understand! If God told you to do something that you did not understand would you do it?

7. The seventh level of obedience is: obeying instructions that go against reason.

Why would God tell you to continue to live on in a country ravaged by poverty and famine when you have the opportunity to live in a prosperous nation? But this is exactly what He told Isaac to do. "And there was a famine in the land, beside the first famine that was in the days of Abraham. And Isaac went unto Abimelech king of the Philistines unto Gerar. The Lord appeared unto him, and said, Go not down into Egypt; dwell in the land which I shall tell thee of: Sojourn in this land" (Genesis 26:1-3).

Today, few Christians would obey the Lord if He told us to leave our wealthy cities and go live in poverty-stricken countries.

It goes against reason to move your family from the safety of America to the dangerous countryside of West Africa.

Even ministers of the gospel do not want their children to become pastors and live in poverty-stricken Ghana, Mali, Guinea or Niger.

Most pastors actually prefer that their children become doctors, lawyers or businessmen in Europe or America, rather than becoming pastors in West Africa. It goes against reason to sentence your precious children to a life in a poverty-stricken, famine-ridden community rather than sending them to a prosperous and well-to-do place.

8. The eighth level of obedience is: obeying instructions that are painfully difficult.

And all the tithe of the land, whether of the seed of the land, or of the fruit of the tree, is the Lord's: it is holy unto the Lord.

Leviticus 27:30

Tithing is a painfully difficult commandment for many Christians. I do not know of anyone who couldn't do with a bit of extra money. Most of us have expenses and bills that exceed our incomes.

It therefore becomes painfully difficult to take ten percent of your income, which is not enough anyway, and give it away for vague church projects. This is why many Christians do not obey the instruction to pay their tithes.

9. The ninth level of obedience is: obeying instructions that make you unpopular.

Pastors and prophets struggle to prophesy and preach things that make them unpopular. Jeremiah complained that false prophets were speaking lies and predicting only good things. When you predict bad things you become unpopular. Nobody likes to hear bad things about the future. Sometimes, to obey the Lord's instructions about what to preach can make you unpopular.

Jeremiah was unpopular because he was predicting bad things all the time. He even countered good prophecies and good predictions that other prophets gave. He said that all those good news prophecies were lies. There is no wonder that Jeremiah was an unpopular prophet. But he was popular with God. His name and his prophecies are included in the Bible. In the end, his unpopular prophecies came to pass and the popular prophets were proved to be false prophets.

> *Then said I, Ah, Lord God! Behold, the prophets say unto them, ye shall not see the sword, neither shall ye have famine; but I will give you assured peace in this place.*
>
> *Then the Lord said unto me, the prophets prophesy lies in my name: I sent them not, neither have I commanded them, neither spake unto them: they prophesy unto you a false vision and divination, and a thing of nought, and the deceit of their heart.*
>
> **Jeremiah 14:13-14**

10. The tenth level of obedience is: obeying instructions that are bizarre.

> *… Every man child among you shall be circumcised. And ye shall circumcise the flesh of your foreskin; and it shall be a token of the covenant betwixt me and you.*
>
> **Genesis 17:10-11**

Most Christians struggle with instructions that make them look silly or bizarre. What is the importance of cutting off the foreskins of every grown man? Indeed, everybody who received this mutilation would be sick and in pain for many days.

Yet, without anaesthesia and without antibiotics Abraham was instructed to do this amazing surgery on every grown man. Abraham obeyed God and made everyone under him carry out this bizarre operation in the desert.

Abraham obeyed God and did what was ridiculous.

This is one of the reasons why Abraham stands out as the father of faith and the father of the obedient ones.

11. The eleventh level of obedience is: obeying instructions that give rise to obvious evils.

Many Christians would struggle with obedience if the Lord instructed us to marry a prostitute. There are so many evils that could come to your life for marrying a prostitute. Hosea could have contracted gonorrhoea, syphilis, herpes simplex or Chlamydia infections by marrying a prostitute. Hosea's prostitute wife could have become unfaithful because he did not meet up to the standards of some of her former customers. What kind of mother would this prostitute be to the children of Hosea? Indeed, this was an instruction fraught with many potential evils. Yet, Hosea obeyed the Lord and married the prostitute God had spoken to him about.

> When the LORD first spoke through Hosea, the LORD said to Hosea, "Go, take to yourself a wife of harlotry and have children of harlotry; for the land commits flagrant harlotry, forsaking the LORD." So he went

> *and took Gomer the daughter of Diblaim, and she conceived and bore him a son.*
>
> **Hosea 1:2-3 (NASB)**

Similarly, many Christians would struggle with an instruction to kill men, women and children.

Yet, as you grow in the Lord, He may actually ask you to do things that may seem harmful to others. Be ready to move to the higher levels of obedience, sometimes doing things that do not make sense to you.

> *Thus saith the Lord of hosts, I remember that which Amalek did to Israel, how he laid wait for him in the way, when he came up from Egypt.*
>
> *Now go and smite Amalek, and utterly destroy all that they have, and spare them not; but slay both man and woman, infant and suckling, ox and sheep, camel and ass.*
>
> **1 Samuel 15:2-3**

12. The twelfth level of obedience is: obeying instructions that may lead to your own death.

> *Then he took unto him the twelve, and said unto them, Behold, we go up to Jerusalem, and all things that are written by the prophets concerning the Son of man shall be accomplished.*
>
> *For he shall be delivered unto the Gentiles, and shall be mocked, and spitefully entreated, and spitted on:*

> *and they shall scourge him, and put him to death: and the third day he shall rise again.*
>
> **Luke 18:31-33**

This is the highest level of obedience; to follow an instruction which you know will lead to your own destruction and death. Jesus followed His father's wishes and went to the cross. There was nothing rational, reasonable or pleasurable about Him being humiliated, tortured and murdered by the vicious soldiers of the brutal Roman Empire.

You must develop yourself spiritually until you are malleable and flexible in His hands. You must be so willing and so obedient that the Lord can ask you to be hungry for His sake.

You must so willing and so obedient that the Lord can ask you to live or to die for His sake.

You must so willing and so obedient that the Lord can ask you to be happy or to accept unhappiness as your lot on this earth!

Chapter 26

Common Alternatives to Obedience

Christians love to do good deeds that impress others. Many of these nice-sounding deeds are often clever alternatives to simple obedience.

Obey the Lord and stop doing all sorts of other things that He has not asked you to do. God will not reward you because you did many good things but because you obeyed Him. Many times, obeying God will not bring you honour from men.

But why do you seek the praise of men? If you please men you cannot please God.

When people are asked to serve God, they come up with nice-sounding alternatives to the real will of God. Below are a few examples of these wise sounding alternatives to practical obedience.

1. Fulfiling family obligations is a common alternative to obeying God.

If any man come to me, and HATE not his father, and mother, and wife, and children, and brethren, and sisters, yea, and his own life also, he cannot be my disciple.

Luke 14:26

One of the common reasons people give for disregarding God's instructions is their family. The Bible is littered with instructions on honouring parents, obeying husbands, loving wives, looking after children and respecting the elderly. These Scriptures have been used by many as a perfect excuse for not following the voice of God. Statements like "God first, family second and ministry third" have been coined to buttress these excuses. But this statement is not in the Bible. It is somebody's idea. The family is important. God is the creator of the family. He will not lead you in a way that will destroy your family.

When the Israelites did not want to obey the Lord, they claimed their children would perish in the desert. Concern for their children was their reason for not following God's will. This excuse really angered the Lord and He made it clear to them when He punished them in the wilderness. He said,

Moreover your little ones, which ye said should be a prey, and your children, which in that day had no

> *knowledge between good and evil, they shall go in thither, and unto them will I give it, and they shall possess it.*
>
> **Deuteronomy 1:39**

Even Jesus had to contend with these family excuses. The people who didn't want to follow Him would use their fathers or the people at home as excuses for not coming along.

But Jesus said you would have to hate your father and mother, brothers and sisters, wife and husband in order to follow Him. Your family must not come before your call. Your family must not prevent you from obeying the call of God.

> *And He said to another, "Follow Me." But he said,*
>
> *"Lord, permit me first to go and bury my father. But He said to him, "Allow the dead to bury their own dead; but as for you, go and proclaim everywhere the kingdom of God."*
>
> *Another also said, "I will follow You, Lord; but first permit me to say good-bye to those at home." But Jesus said to him, "No one, after putting his hand to the plow and looking back, is fit for the kingdom of God."*
>
> **Luke 9:59-62 (NASB)**

2. Listening to your wife is a common alternative to obeying God.

And unto Adam he said, Because thou hast hearkened unto the voice of thy wife...

Genesis 3:17

... And Abram hearkened to the voice of Sarai...

Genesis 16:2

The two biggest problems of this world have come about through men of authority listening to their wives rather than obeying God. Your wife's voice is not the same as the voice of God.

Wives are gentle, sweet and look harmless but that is not a good enough reason to set aside the voice of God and do what they say.

God is not a woman!

God is not a wife!

Your wife is not God!

Please remember this! Follow God and you will be blessed.

Follow your wife and you may end up with a big curse.

Go and ask Abraham what happened to him.

Go and ask Adam what happened to him.

My wife knows that I greatly desire to follow God even if it means not following her wishes.

Because the Bible teaches us to love our wives, many ministers feel great pressure to always listen to their wives and somehow please them. This can be a great trap and lead to your downfall. It led to the downfall of Adam and we are all paying the price of one leader listening to his wife instead of listening to God.

This mistake also led to the downfall of Abraham. And today, we are all paying the price for the world conflict that Abraham created through listening to his wife.

If you are leader or a man of authority, you must be especially careful about the pressure that comes to bear on you from your wife. Be careful that you don't lead your whole ministry down the path of ruin because of your wife's voice.

Obeying your wife will never be a good enough substitute for your obedience to the voice of God.

3. Raising money in the name of God and for His work is a common alternative to obeying God.

> *Wherefore then didst thou not obey the voice of the Lord, but didst fly upon the spoil, and didst evil in the sight of the Lord?*
>
> **I Samuel 15:19**

Saul spared the goats and the sheep and raised some much-needed money for the Kingdom of God. Indeed Saul's disobedience raised a good income for the people of God. The spoil would feed the soldiers and make the troops happy. Yet God was not impressed with the money even though it was income for His house.

It is amazing how decisions for the work of God are deemed to be right only if they are financially profitable.

Doing financially profitable things is not the same as obeying God. Obeying God may be financially profitable but obeying God may be financially very unprofitable. It is entirely up to what the Lord wants.

Many people feel that once money is raised and a good income is achieved for God's work, the will of God has been done. In fact, many ministers measure their success by the offerings they get. This is a very dangerous practice because being successful and being prosperous does not mean you are in the will of God.

A wicked and rebellious pastor once showed me a gift that he had received from a wealthy Christian. He pointed out to me that God was with him and God was actually helping him to be as wicked as he was.

He said, "This gift shows that God is with me and that He is pleased with what I am doing." But I didn't think so. I didn't think that God was with him and I didn't think that God supported his misdeeds.

It is sad that he received his assurance of being in the will of God by the fact that money was flowing into his ministry.

4. Showing compassion to people is a common alternative to obeying God.

And at that time came Joshua, and cut off the Anakims from the mountains, from Hebron, from Debir, from Anab, and from all the mountains of Judah, and from all the mountains of Israel: Joshua destroyed them utterly with their cities.

THERE WAS NONE OF THE ANAKIMS LEFT in the land of the children of Israel: ONLY IN GAZA, IN GATH, AND IN ASHDOD, THERE REMAINED.

Joshua 11:21-22

No one is wiser than God and no one is more compassionate than God.

There are many people who engage in different acts of compassion and feel that these deeds are a good substitute for obeying God. Instead of doing exactly what God says they find something impressive and compassionate to do. Instead of paying tithes you will find people giving their money to poor people or to the sick.

Joshua showed compassion to the cities of Gaza, Gath and Ashdod. He did not kill all the Philistines there but left them alive in direct disobedience to God's clear instructions. Many years later, the disobedience bore fruit. These three cities, which were not wiped out by Joshua, produced the bitterest enemies of the children of Israel.

Gath produced Goliath who fought against Israel. "And there went out a champion out of the camp of the Philistines, named Goliath, of Gath, whose height was six cubits and a span" (1 Samuel 17:4).

Gaza produced the harlot that destroyed Samson. "Then went Samson to Gaza, and saw there an harlot, and went in unto her" (Judges 16:1).

Ashdod was the city which captured the ark of God and put it in the temple of Dagon. "And the Philistines took the ark of God, and brought it from Eben-ezer unto Ashdod. When the Philistines took the ark of God, they brought it into the house of Dagon, and set it by Dagon" (1 Samuel 5:2).

Make sure you are not kinder than God.

Make sure that you are not more compassionate than God Himself.

Make sure that you are not more loving than Jesus. There is something wrong with your love and compassion when a sinful person like you is praised as being kinder than God!

5. Making sacrifices which God has not asked for is a common alternative to obeying God.

> *To what purpose is the multitude of your sacrifices unto me? saith the LORD.*
>
> **Isaiah 1:11**

The Bible has many examples of people making sacrifices which God did not ask for. King Saul, Nadab and Abihu are just a few examples of people who made sacrifices that God did not want.

These sacrifices actually irritated the Lord because they were such a big hypocritical show of unreal worship.

God is not pleased with these sacrifices even though men are impressed. God is not deceived with the show of sacrifice and humility. God always prefers obedience to any form of sacrifice.

> *"And Samuel said, Hath the LORD as great delight in burnt offerings and sacrifices, as in obeying the voice of the LORD? Behold, to obey is better than sacrifice, and to hearken than the fat of rams."*
>
> **1 Samuel 15:22**

You can lose your life when you make sacrifices you have not been asked to make. Ask Nadab and Abihu what happened to them when they made sacrifices they had not been asked to make. "And Nadab and Abihu, the sons of Aaron, took either of them his censer, and put fire therein, and put incense thereon, and offered strange fire before the Lord, which he commanded them not. And there went out fire from the LORD, and devoured them, and they died before the Lord" (Leviticus 10:1-2).

Even in the New Testament, born-again Christians get a feeling of righteousness when they make certain sacrifices and take themselves through hardships. Many times, God does not require you to go through hardships. All He requires from you is simple obedience.

Fasting to Death

One day, whilst fasting, I collapsed to the ground wondering if I could get up again. I called on the Lord to save my life. I didn't want to die. But the Lord simply reminded me that He had not asked me to take myself through those hardships. I was fasting in that way because it had been my tradition for many years to give my body severe treatment.

Each year, as I treated my body harshly I felt more powerful and more righteous. But the Bible is very clear that severe treatment of the body does not make you righteous and does not even help you to overcome the flesh.

Do not handle, do not taste, do not touch! ...

> *These are matters which have, to be sure, the appearance of wisdom in self-made religion and self-abasement and SEVERE TREATMENT OF THE BODY, but are of no value against fleshly indulgence.*
> **Colossians 2:21, 23 (NASB)**

We love to do things that make us feel righteous. "For not knowing about God's righteousness, and seeking to establish their own, they did not subject themselves to the righteousness of God" (Romans 10:3, NASB).

Paul tells us how to overcome our fleshly desires without maltreating our bodies. This is a great key to overcoming in this life. Overcoming your fleshly impulses will happen as you set your affection on things above and seek things that are above and not things that are on this earth (Colossians 3:1-3).

Chapter 27

The Promises and Blessings for Obedience

How Can I Be Blessed?

There are three main ways by which a blessing can come to your life. The first is by being born into a blessed family. Blessings tend to flow through family lines. Another way you can receive a blessing is by being associated with a blessed person. The third way you can be blessed is by being obedient to God.

Blessings that follow obedience are more predictable and determinable by you. You can cause certain blessings to come into your life by being obedient to God. In this chapter, I want you to learn, to understand and to believe in the power of obedience to the Word of God.

All through the Bible, all those who obeyed God were blessed super-abundantly because of their obedience. Obedience is the key to the blessings of God!

Seven Direct Promises for Obedience

1. You will become a peculiar treasure through obedience.

> *Now therefore, if ye will obey my voice indeed, and keep my covenant, then ye shall BE A PECULIAR TREASURE unto me above all people: for all the earth is mine:*
>
> **Exodus 19:5**

2. It will be well with you and your children because of your obedience.

> *O that there were such an heart in them, that they would fear me, and keep all my commandments always, that IT MIGHT BE WELL WITH THEM, and with their children for ever!*
>
> **Deuteronomy 5:29**

3. Your days will be lengthened through obedience to the Holy Spirit.

> *And if thou wilt walk in my ways, to keep my statutes and my commandments, as thy father David did walk, then I will LENGTHEN THY DAYS.*
>
> **1 Kings 3:14**

4. **You will be blessed in all your undertakings through obedience.**

   But whoso looketh into the perfect law of liberty, and continueth therein, he being not a forgetful hearer, but a doer of the work, this man shall be BLESSED IN HIS DEED.

   James 1:25

5. **You will have access to the tree of life because of your obedience.**

   Blessed are they that do his commandments, that they may have right to the tree of life, and may enter in through the gates into the city.

   Revelation 22:14

6. **You will be blessed with good health because of your obedience.**

   And said, If thou wilt diligently hearken to the voice of the LORD thy God, and wilt do that which is right in his sight, and wilt give ear to his commandments, and keep all his statutes, I will put NONE OF THESE DISEASES UPON THEE, which I have brought upon the Egyptians: for I am the LORD that healeth thee.

   Exodus 15:26

7. You will be blessed with increase because of your obedience.

In that I command you today to love the LORD your God, to walk in His ways and to keep His commandments and His statutes and His judgments, that you may LIVE AND MULTIPLY, and that the LORD your God may bless you in the land where you are entering to possess it.

Deuteronomy 30:16 (NASB)

Four Direct Blessings for Obedience

1. Obeying the voice of God gives rise to the blessing of a worldwide and everlasting ministry.

Not everyone has a worldwide ministry. Some people have ministries to their communities. Others have ministries to their nations.

Others have ministries that go to all the nations of the world. Perhaps God will give you a worldwide ministry if you obey him in the way Abraham did.

Now THE LORD HAD SAID UNTO ABRAM, GET THEE OUT OF THY COUNTRY, and from thy kindred, and from thy father's house, unto a land that I will shew thee: and I will make of thee a great nation, and I will bless thee, and make thy name great; and thou shalt be a blessing:

And I will bless them that bless thee, and curse him that curseth thee: and in thee shall all families of the earth be blessed.

SO ABRAM DEPARTED, AS THE LORD HAD SPOKEN UNTO HIM...

Genesis 12:1-4

And I will make thy seed to multiply as the stars of heaven, and will give unto thy seed all these countries; and in thy seed shall all the nations of the earth be blessed;

BECAUSE THAT ABRAHAM OBEYED MY VOICE, AND KEPT MY CHARGE, MY COMMANDMENTS, MY STATUTES, AND MY LAWS.

Genesis 26:4-5

2. Obeying the voice of God gives rise to the blessing of greatness.

Perhaps you have desired to prosper and perhaps you have done many things to make yourself great. But the only person who can really make you great is the Lord.

Do not be envious of people who become great through their obedience to God. Do not pity people who are obeying God. Do not feel sorry for those who have given their lives for the gospel. Their obedience will lead to greatness! Isaac obeyed the Lord and became a great man.

And there was a famine in the land, beside the first famine that was in the days of Abraham. And Isaac went unto Abimelech king of the Philistines unto Gerar.

And the Lord appeared unto him, and said, Go not down into Egypt; dwell in the land which I shall tell thee of:

Sojourn in this land, and I will be with thee, and will bless thee; for unto thee, and unto thy seed, I will give all these countries, and I will perform the oath which I sware unto Abraham thy father;

And I will make thy seed to multiply as the stars of heaven, and will give unto thy seed all these countries; and in thy seed shall all the nations of the earth be blessed;

Genesis 26:1-4

Then Isaac sowed in that land, and received in the same year an hundredfold: and the Lord blessed him

And THE MAN WAXED GREAT, AND WENT FORWARD, AND GREW UNTIL HE BECAME VERY GREAT: for he had possession of flocks, and possessions of herds, and great store of servants: and the Philistines envied him.

Genesis 26:12-14

3. Obeying the voice of God releases the blessings of long life, riches and honour.

The Scriptures show how David endeavoured to obey the Lord as much as he could. He was human and he failed in the matter of Uriah the Hittite. But he did ALL THE WILL of God and received the blessings of the Lord.

David ended up full of riches, full of honour! Unfortunately, this cannot be said about the end of everybody. Many of us end up disgraced, poverty-stricken and with shortened lives. Mercy! May God give us the grace to pursue obedience to His perfect will so that our end will be like the end of David – full of days, riches and honour.

> *And he walked in all the sins of his father, which he had done before him: and his heart was not perfect with the Lord his God, as the heart of David his father.*
>
> *Nevertheless for David's sake did the Lord his God give him a lamp in Jerusalem, to set up his son after him, and to establish Jerusalem:*
>
> *Because DAVID DID THAT WHICH WAS RIGHT IN THE EYES OF THE LORD, AND TURNED NOT ASIDE FROM ANY THING THAT HE COMMANDED HIM ALL THE DAYS OF HIS LIFE, SAVE ONLY IN THE MATTER OF URIAH THE HITTITE.*
>
> 1 Kings 15:3-5

After these things He gave them judges until Samuel the prophet.

Then they asked for a king, and God gave them Saul the son of Kish, a man of the tribe of Benjamin, for forty years.

After He had removed him, He raised up David to be their king, concerning whom He also testified and said, I HAVE FOUND DAVID the son of Jesse, A MAN AFTER MY HEART, WHO WILL DO ALL MY WILL.

Acts 13:20-22 (NASB)

And he died in a good old age, FULL OF DAYS, RICHES, AND HONOUR: and Solomon his son reigned in his stead.

1 Chronicles 29:28

4. Obeying the voice of God releases the blessing of the presence of God.

Jesus answered and said unto him, IF A MAN LOVE ME, HE WILL KEEP MY WORDS: and my Father will love him, and WE WILL COME UNTO HIM, AND MAKE OUR ABODE WITH HIM.

John 14:23

Perhaps, this is the greatest blessing of obedience – the presence of God. Indeed, great blessings are promised to the disciples who obey the voice of Jesus.

As you watch and listen to different preachers, you will notice a difference in doctrine. But you will also realise a difference in the extent to which they have the presence of God. Watch out for it and you will surely notice it if you are sensitive to the Spirit.

Jesus said: "We will come to him and make our abode with him!" This is a description of God's presence being manifest with the disciples. God is everywhere. We know He is omnipotent. So when Jesus says, "we will come to him and make our abode with him" He speaks of a greater presence of the Father and of the Son.

Jesus promises to come and dwell in you and with you if you obey Him: this is the promise of the presence of God.

There is a *presence* and an *aura* around people who are obeying God. This presence and this aura is not found around people who are not obeying God's voice.

People may preach the Word of God and have good doctrines but there is a certain presence of God that needs to be there! Do you not want to have the presence of God in your life and ministry? Learn to obey the voice of God even if it doesn't make sense.

Obey Him because obeying Him brings the presence of God into what you are doing!

Dag Heward-Mills, an author of several best-selling books, also founded Lighthouse Chapel International, which has become a worldwide denomination. His radio, TV and internet programs reach millions around the world. Other outreaches include conferences for pastors and ministers, and the renowned Anagkoazo Bible Ministry & Training Centre.

One night, whilst still a medical student, the Lord anointed Dag Heward-Mills as he waited on Him in a remote town of Ghana. He was supernaturally anointed and heard the words, "From now on you can teach..."

This supernatural call is what has ushered him into a worldwide ministry.

Today, his Healing Jesus Crusades are conducted throughout the world with thousands in attendance and many accompanying miracles. These phenomenal miracles, attested to by medical doctors, have included the opening of the eyes of the blind, the restoring of hearing to the deaf, the emptying of wheelchairs, and even the raising of the dead.

www.daghewardmills.org

email : evangelist@daghewardmills.org

MORE BOOKS BY DAG HEWARD-MILLS

LOYALTY SERIES
- Fathers and Loyalty
- Leaders and Loyalty
- Loyalty and Disloyalty
- Those Who Accuse You
- Those Who Forget
- Those Who Leave You
- Those Who Pretend

CHURCHBUILDING SERIES
- Church Growth
- Church Planting
- The Mega Church (2nd Ed)

ANOINTING SERIES
- Catch the Anointing
- Ministering with Signs and Wonders
- Steps to the Anointing

PASTORAL MINISTRY SERIES
- The Art of Leadership (2nd Ed.)
- The Art of Shepherding
- Transform Your Pastoral Ministry

WORK OF MINISTRY SERIES
- How You Can Be in the Perfect Will of God
- Losing, Suffering, Sacrificing, Dying
- Many are Called
- Proton
- Rules of Church Work
- Rules of Full-Time Ministry

SUCCESS SERIES
- Why Non-Tithing Christians Become Poor and How Tithing Christians Can Become Rich

CHRISTIAN LIFE SERIES
- Backsliding
- Daughter, You Can Make It
- Demons and How to Deal with Them
- Model Marriage
- Name it! Claim it! Take it!
- Quiet Time
- Tell Them

SUNPENNY PUBLISHING GROUP

ROSE & CROWN, BLUE JEANS, BOATHOOKS, SUNBERRY, CHRISTLIGHT, and EPTA Books

MORE BOOKS FROM CHRISTLIGHT and ROSE & CROWN BOOKS (CHRISTIAN):

A Devil's Ransom, by Adele Jones
Blue Freedom, by Sandra Peut
Bridge to Nowhere, by Stephanie Parker McKean
Embracing Change, by Debbie Roome
Going Astray, by Christine Moore
My Sea is Wide, by Rowland Evans
Redemption on Red River, by Cheryl R Cain
Summer Love, Winter Tears, by Carol Collins
Uncharted Waters, by Sara DuBose

MORE BOOKS FROM the SUNPENNY GROUP
www.sunpenny.com

A Little Book of Pleasures, by William Wood
Blackbirds Baked in a Pie, by Eugene Barter
Breaking the Circle, by Althea Barr
Dance of Eagles, by JS Holloway
Don't Pass Me By, by Julie McGowan
Far Out, by Corinna Weyreter
Fish Soup, by Michelle Heatley
Just One More Summer, by Julie McGowan
Someday, Maybe, by Jenny Piper
The Mountains Between, by Julie McGowan

Lightning Source UK Ltd.
Milton Keynes UK
UKHW011551030820
367624UK00002B/564

9 781909 278783